Your Towns and Cities in the

Reading
in the Great War
1914–1916

Your Towns and Cities in the Great War

Reading
in the Great War
1914–1916

David Bilton

Pen & Sword
MILITARY

First published in Great Britain in 2016 by
PEN & SWORD MILITARY
an imprint of
Pen and Sword Books Ltd
47 Church Street
Barnsley
South Yorkshire S70 2AS

ISBN 978 1 78346 219 3

A CIP record for this book is available from the British Library

Printed and bound in England
by CPI Group (UK) Ltd, Croydon, CR0 4YY

Typeset in Times New Roman by Chic Graphics

Pen & Sword Books Ltd incorporates the imprints of
Pen & Sword Archaeology, Atlas, Aviation, Battleground, Discovery,
Family History, History, Maritime, Military, Naval, Politics, Railways,
Select, Social History, Transport, True Crime, Claymore Press,
Frontline Books, Leo Cooper, Praetorian Press, Remember When,
Seaforth Publishing and Wharncliffe.

For a complete list of Pen and Sword titles please contact
Pen and Sword Books Limited
47 Church Street, Barnsley, South Yorkshire, S70 2AS, England
E-mail: enquiries@pen-and-sword.co.uk
Website: www.pen-and-sword.co.uk

Contents

Acknowledgements

As with previous books, a great big thank you to Anne Coulson for her help in checking the text and to the staff of Reading Central Library for their help, kindness and knowledge during the gestation of this book. While many of the illustrations are from contemporary newspapers I am very grateful to Mike Armitage, Julie Cox, Andrew French of the Berkshire Yeomanry Museum, Maurice Johnson, Mike Paul, Liz Tait and Richard van Emden for providing further information and photographs. Errors of omission or commission are mine alone.

Introduction

This book is about Reading, though it is difficult to say exactly what Reading encompasses. As a borough council it comprised Reading, Caversham, Coley, parts of old Earley, Southcote, Tilehurst and Whitley, but as the county town of Berkshire its influence and importance spread across the whole county. I have therefore occasionally included the immediate outlying towns and villages to provide a flavour of life in both urban and rural Berkshire during the war. Keen-eyed readers will no doubt see many similarities between then and now and between any of the war years and conclude that in reality only relatively trivial matters change. Life is, after all, life. And some careful readers may well discover that what was presented in wartime as definite fact was not actually so. Caveat lector.

Berks Terriers – Summer Camp 1913 and the men clean up their equipment. A year later they would be rushed from camp to move to their war station.

Berkshire is the Royal County; had a royal regiment and the monarch's official residence is Windsor. However, this title was not official until 1957, though it had been in widespread use for about thirty years when the Great War started. Regardless of officialdom, all the residents had felt themselves to be living in the Royal County since Victorian times.

Berkshire was, and still is, especially in the west, a predominantly agricultural county with some industry in the towns. Reading was traditionally famous for its 3 Bs: biscuits (Huntley & Palmers), beer (Simonds) and bulbs (Suttons Seeds), but there were really 5 Bs, with the inclusion of boxes (Huntley, Bourne and Stevens) and bricks (Colliers). Of these the biggest employer was Huntley and Palmers. More than 5,000 people were employed by them; their annual holiday excursion resulted in all Reading schools closing because so few children were not part of it.

July 16th and the Licensed Victuallers of Reading enjoy a day trip to Dorchester for afternoon tea.

In the rural west, farm labourers and servants were still hired at the Michaelmas hiring fair, but, in the towns, labour moved more freely and there were often disputes between employers and employees. The traditional craftsmen would have been surprised to know that they, as well as those in agriculture, unknown to them, would play a part in the war effort. Osier (willow) rods were used to make basket shell containers and invalid chairs. To replace shaving brush handles previously obtained from Germany, the Turnery Works in Thatcham supplied thousands while another firm made mop handles for the navy.

Reading also proudly boasted a University College, at which Wilfred Owen studied while he was working in Dunsden Green, and one of the oldest boys' schools in the country, both of which would provide numbers of officers for the New Armies. As well as hosting and training many thousands of troops from across the country, the town was also home to two Royal Flying Corps units. Two fields

Sergeant Dallimore of Prospect Street, was a pre-war regular soldier who had been seconded to the New Zealand Army. He would return to his home after the war as an officer.

in Coley Park were used as an airfield for the Royal Flying Corps, No. 1 School of Military Aeronautics and No. 1 School of Technical Training, based nearby. However, flying was disrupted by river fogs and by the end of the war the airfield fell into disuse.

Reading was and still is an important part of the nation's transport system. It was a major staging point on the old Bath Road (A4) from London to Bath and Bristol; it is on two navigable rivers, the Kennet and Thames, and was a major railway town. The central station on the Great Western mainline doubled as the terminus for the London and South Western and the South Eastern Railway. It was therefore easily accessible from most other important towns and cities in the south and midlands.

Reading produced four newspapers, all weeklies – the *Chronicle*, the *Observer*, the *Mercury* and the *Standard*, each with its own style. The bestselling paper was the *Chronicle* which provided a front page of small ads, followed by local articles with some pictures, and a leader about current affairs. The *Standard* was shorter and provided a mix of

Reg Paul, on the left, taken before the war, when he was training as a cabinet maker.

photographs and stories, the *Observer* and the *Mercury* were very traditional and purely text. This book is based on the contemporary articles in these papers.

What was life like in Reading in the days immediately preceding the war? The following excerpts from the July 1914 newspapers show that there was no thought of war before the leader in the issue of 31 July. Everything continued as usual, and in some respects it still does, though we see that some aspects of pre-war life have long gone:

The Henry Lucas hospital in Wokingham advertised a vacancy for a poor man. The position was open to any 'poor man born in or for at least three years an inhabitant of one of the following parishes in the county of Berkshire, viz., Wokingham Parish,

Wokingham town, Arborfield, Finchampstead, New Windsor, East Hampstead, Clewer, Old Windsor, Barkham, Binfield, Hurst, Ruscombe, Sandhurst, Winkfield, Swallowfield, Sunninghill or Bray.' In order to receive the £25 per annum, £2 fuel allowance and use of a partly-furnished room, the man had to 'be over 50, of sober life and conversation, poor and impotent (and) decayed in estate by sickness or other infirmity.' It was a position for life unless they became senile, a nuisance or a danger, in which case they would be evicted.

Sport, crime, military manoeuvres and general summer activities filled most of the papers every week. Although they were produced in Reading, their readership stretched over Berkshire, hence they covered stories across the county.

Stories in the month preceding the war included the Royal Berkshire Regiment cricket team beating Basildon, 160 runs to 77, with Sergeant Taylor being the highest scorer with 55 runs. It being July, there was of course the Henley Regatta to report, and the annual sports day at Rushmoor recreation ground for 1 Battalion Royal Berkshire Regiment.

Among the numerous reports on garden fêtes there was the annual Reading Show where Mr. E.D. Marshall was awarded first prize for his Sweet Peas in the section for amateurs residing in Reading who did not regularly employ a professional gardener. At the Burghfield and Sulhampstead Flower Show, the first prize for Shelled Peas was won by G. Richards, A. Woodford took first prize in the category 'Nosegay of wild flowers and grasses' for boys, and Norah West took the girls' prize. Mrs F. Pembroke took the prize for the best darning and the best workman's dinner was made by Mrs J.D. Whitburn. The period also saw the start of a major infrastructure project, the Tilehurst sewerage mains. Shortly after the commencement of digging work was affected by a strike demanding parity with council workers, a raise of a halfpenny an hour, from 5½d to 6d, and a wartime manpower shortage as reservists were called to the colours.

While Austria attacked Serbia, and France, Germany and Russia started their preparations for the coming war, the Reading press concentrated on local military activity:

Reservists reporting at the barracks.

On Salisbury Plain, a camp of military aircraft was visited by Lord Roberts and foreign military attaches. At King's Meadow in Reading there was a review of the National Reserve; the British Red Cross VAD and the HQ Company of 4 (TF) Battalion Royal Berkshire Regiment spent an enjoyable afternoon at Major Cooper's mother's house where they were awarded prizes and provided with refreshments.

At Eton, the school training corps was inspected by Major General Davies who 'noted dirty boots and too much hair about. Long hair might be alright for men called "Nuts" but it had nothing to do with soldiers. It was not soldier-like.' Fortunately by the time of their next inspection at annual camp, two weeks later, they looked smart and shorn.

In Wokingham, H Company of 4 (TF) Battalion continued its training programme with an emphasis on getting all men to complete their musketry training. This was in anticipation of the big military event that would happen over July and August when an estimated 30-40,000 Territorials and Officer Training Corps members would be under canvas on Salisbury Plain. Men would be arriving from all over the country for the exercises. The centre-point would be the arrival of three semi-local territorial divisions – the Wessex, 2nd London and Home Counties.

The most famous statue in Reading, the Maiwand Lion, which commemorates the losses of the Berkshire Regiment during the Afghan campaign of 1879-1880. The memorial for the Great War is at the entrance to Forbury Gardens.

In such a parochial town, deaths and court proceedings across the county were given much coverage. No crime was too small to report if there was space – cycle stealing, horse theft, riding without lights, swearing in public, domestic violence, drunkenness, changing the year on a birth certificate to get their son out of school a year earlier, and breaking and entering – these were just some of the crimes covered.

During the month there was an inquest on a young driver killed in a railway accident. Much excitement was caused by a chase across Prospect Park when the park keeper tried to apprehend a thief. The Stop Press of one edition was a drowning in the River Kennet. In another, the biggest story covered the accidental death of two people in a punting accident at Pangbourne.

Excessive alcohol consumption was the cause of many cases heard by magistrates. Often it resulted in poor behaviour, other times in poor driving. On one occasion, a drunk driving down West Street mounted the pavement and nearly knocked three women down. The driver was fined 40 shillings for drunkenness and £10 for dangerous driving. And as always there were disputes between neighbours. In Swallowfield Mrs Jennings was bound over to keep the peace and fined £2 with costs of eight shillings and six pence. Her crime was throwing a bucket of water over her neighbour who was sitting resting in the garden.

The Chief Constable's report detailed the level of crime in the borough over the quarter ending 31 March:

Indictable offences:

Number of crimes committed	81
Persons proceeded against	64
Committed for trial	22
Convicted summarily	15
Probation, sent to Industrial School, dismissed, withdrawn, abandoned, on bail	17
Non-indictable offences:	
Number of persons proceeded against	406
Convicted	302
Probation, bound over, dismissed, withdrawn	80
Army or Navy offences	15
Committed to prison to await trial at Quarter Sessions as incorrigible rogues	3

Two final pieces of news set the scene for Reading in the Great War, a town whose experiences mirrored many elsewhere but which were at the same time specific – it was a small county town in rural Berkshire, neither wholly urban or set in the countryside. It was a town with one foot in each setting.

Reading was experiencing a heat wave with highs of 79°F and lows of 55°F. The resulting drought reduced the rate at which grass grew, causing reduced milk production. Readers were warned to expect price rises as a result.

It was not always negative news that was reported. Workers at the

Huntley, Bourne and Stevens factory had cause to celebrate. They were to have their working hours cut from 54 to 50 hours after the August Bank Holiday with no reduction in wages and they were to start an hour-and-a-half later at 8 a.m.

Unlike the town we know today, pre-Great War Reading was not an affluent place. Research undertaken in 1912 recorded that the average wage for a week's work for men over twenty years of age was about 24 shillings and 6 pence. Compared to the rest of the country, this was judged by the researchers as being relatively very low. The main reason for Reading's marked poverty was this low average wage. The wages of unskilled labour in Reading were insufficient to support a family of three or more children. Poor or not, many workers rushed to join the colours when the war started.

In this narrative there are stories of great heroism, patriotism, and duty, and, at the other end of the spectrum of life, petty squabbles, drunkenness, incest and murder. Life does not follow a linear path. The trivial and the deeply serious exist side-by-side, hand in hand.

Reading Town Hall from Friar Street.

Sometimes the stories in this book are chronological, at other times grouped, related, linked across the year. In some cases they are one-offs, perhaps they stand alone, sometimes they are visited again in a different context. They may be flippant, serious, statistical, trivial or of no apparent consequence. That they appear after each other is in no way meant to detract from the personal and national struggle they portray.

National papers provided international and national news, and the local papers explained how and what local people felt. Life is a messy business; the local papers gave a warts-and-all view of real life, with no air-brushing. What I gleaned from local papers is a picture of daily life, the experience of many reflecting how they saw the war, how they behaved and what they felt at the highest, lowest, saddest and happiest times in their war. I have tried to show that normal life in Reading was often mundane, that the war, while being all-pervasive, often touched people's lives, with the exception of death and disability, only in transient, temporary ways. In many cases there seemed to be no war going on because nothing had really changed, or was the situation just slightly different? If you were already hungry, how would rationing affect you? If you had no job, no shelter, how were you affected? On the other hand, what did you do if you found yourself pregnant and you weren't married, and the father is in France or perhaps your father? The answers are to be found somewhere in the following pages.

CHAPTER 1

1914
Eager for a Fight

Although the phrase 'the shot heard round the world' refers to the American Revolution, it is as accurate to apply it to the shots fired by 19-year-old Gavrilo Princip in Sarajevo. But neither France nor Russia saw the incident as a reason to 'imperil the new climate of confidence. Germany, they considered, could only be bluffing in supporting the Austrian demarche against Serbia.'

A war in the Balkans would surely be of no consequence to the inhabitants of Great Britain. Although 'the apocalyptic climax to the age of European…imperialism' was only a few weeks away, people carried on as usual with their lives. While the inhabitants of Berkshire were aware of these events from the national dailies, the local papers focussed their attentions on other, less weighty matters.

It was a warm summer and people had important things on their minds: holidays. The front page of Berkshire's largest circulation paper, the *Berkshire Chronicle*, established for one hundred and forty-four years, carried its usual mix of classifieds, adverts and news articles. On the front page were auction sales, businesses for sale and properties to let. There were also travel adverts for cheap Third Class excursions to the Royal Agricultural Show at Shrewsbury, or, for those just wanting a break, the GWR was offering holiday excursions to a myriad of places including South Wales, Dublin, Llandudno, Scarborough and Hull. Closer to home, there were weekend specials to London, Southampton and Winchester.

There were also adverts to induce adventurous Readingensians to leave the mother country. Young women were wanted for domestic work in Canada while Australia wanted young men, those very men the country would soon need. 'Lads! Lads! Lads! To Australia for £3. The happiest, healthiest life for British Lads, from 16 to 20 Years, is on big prosperous farms in New South Wales and Victoria. No experience needed, job guaranteed by government, wages start from 10 shillings to 15 shillings weekly. Free board and lodging, quick increases.' How many were enticed to leave Reading by such adverts is not recorded, but there were regular pieces throughout the war about Reading men serving with Empire forces. The number was probably not inconsiderable. Between the years 1901-1910, the annual rate of emigration was 284,000 and for the three years preceding the war it was 464,000 per year – this out of a population of 45 million in 1911.

In its leader for the 31 July edition, the paper finally acknowledged that there could be a problem on the horizon. 'There is no room for doubt that the PM's statement that the European situation was one of "extreme gravity" represents the obvious truth.' However, like most people, the writer was hoping it would stay where it was – in the Balkans. 'If the area of conflict can be limited to those countries (Austria-Hungary and Serbia) the worst may be averted. But, unfortunately, there is the grave danger of the first class powers becoming involved, and if one comes into the conflict it appears that

Watching the mobilisation of the territorials.

Territorials in Dixon's Meadow, Reading waiting for orders to move to the East Coast.

all will, willy-nilly, be dragged into it, because of the alliances known as the Triple Alliance and the Triple Entente.' The remainder of the column is spent on the Irish problem. In a similar vein, another local paper, the *Berks & Oxon Advertiser*, wrote that 'the greater part of Europe seems to have gone mad on war, and England is almost the only Great Power that retains its sanity.'

On Sunday, 2 August, there was a rush for the special editions of the national papers that reported Germany's invasion of France. The next day, Bank Holiday, 3 August, Reading, like the rest of Britain, attempted to enjoy the day off 'but under the direful shadow of the war clouds (it) lost some of its customary gaiety, the customary popular spirit of light-heartedness seemed to be held in check. Nevertheless the crowds at the fetes and other attractions in the neighbourhood were as large as ever, and availed themselves of every opportunity to display their patriotism.' At one fete, 'after listening to a speech by the Borough Member, the great gathering joined in fervently singing "Rule Britannia", and then gave three ringing cheers for the King.' There were equally hearty demonstrations elsewhere across the town and county.

Not everyone cheered. Reading Socialists could see no possible

Troop mobilisation along Friar Street.

justification for a war that would set back the movement and increase the profits of politically influential men at the expense of the lives of working class men. Members should throw in their lot with the International Peace Party and unite under the Red Flag to end war by abolishing capitalism.

In Europe the war had begun but Britain was not yet part of it. That night 'in their eagerness to know what was Germany's reply to England's ultimatum, hundreds of people assembled outside the Post Office in Broad Street…and remained there until the early hours of the morning'. At 11pm, when the German government did not respond to the British Ultimatum, Britain was at war with Germany.

Most of Reading woke to an extra day's holiday in a country at war. They also found the banks closed until the end of the week. In London, the Stock Exchange was closed, to re-open only in January. In Reading, the war immediately dampened sales: 'shopkeepers, except those who sell provisions, are doing little trade' and at some factories and workshops short time was immediately put in place. But, fuelled by the needs of the army, the biscuit trade boomed.

The *Reading Mercury* reported the feeling in Reading: 'In common with every city and town under the British flag, Reading has been

Captain Wilson's audience at the Unionist fete at Erleigh Court were told that the country should offer a united front.

stirred to the depths by the course which the international situation has taken during the last few days, and is reviewing the outlook with profound interest and intense anxiety.'

The recall of military personnel, as elsewhere in the country, started before the commencement of hostilities. 'For the Bank Holiday week-end quite a large number of sailors in Reading and neighbourhood had returned to their homes for their holidays. These and the Naval Reservists left Reading station on Sunday and Monday for Portsmouth and Devonport. Within a few days the borough police force had had twenty reservists called up, seventeen by the army and three by the navy.'

Members of the 4th Battalion were away on their annual camp, 3 August was their first night away. They had retired to their tents when they were woken by a car arriving at speed. By 6.30 am they were at their headquarters in Reading. The newly-arrived special editions of the London papers were avidly read. At 7.20 pm the battalion received orders to mobilise. The news spread quickly by car and bicycle. In pouring rain, in sodden uniforms, men from all over Berkshire assembled and converged on Reading, to await further orders. By

The 1st/4th Royal Berks outside Reading Town Hall prior to entraining for Portsmouth, its mobilisation station

Berkshire Yeomanry waiting for orders at Yeomanry House.

evening, 800 of them left by train for their war-station near Portsmouth, leaving behind two officers and sixty-five men to receive their transport from the remount depot. A spectator was heard to comment as 'the leaden clouds lifted and the sun set in a golden glory as the first company of the "Terriers" entered the station' that this was 'a happy augury for their momentous mission'.

The 1st/4th Battalion leaving Reading.

Yeomanry on the march along King's Road.

Kit inspection on Friar Street for the Berkshire Yeomanry.

The Berkshire Yeomanry on the march along Great Knollys Street.

After three days of training, they moved to Swindon to join up with the other battalions of the 'South Midland Division', later the 48th Division. A few days later they were invited to volunteer for foreign service and by the end of the month were stationed at Chelmsford.

Many other Territorials were also mobilised. At Yeomanry House, the Berkshire Yeomanry grouped before moving off to their war station. In other parts of the county, men had joined the closest unit, regardless of its territorial affiliation. While the Berkshire territorials would have to wait many months before going abroad, the Queen's Own Oxfordshire Hussars would be the first territorials to be involved in the fighting. Eight miles north of Reading, C Squadron in Henley-on-Thames, contained many Berkshire men. D Squadron was led by Winston Churchill's brother, Major John Strange Spencer-Churchill. By 21 September, they were in France and a week later at Hazebrouck.

Change came quickly. Bank notes for ten shillings and one pound were suddenly issued, exchangeable at the Bank of England for gold. Postal Orders became legal tender and banks were given powers to disallow the withdrawal of gold for hoarding, but cash would be available for wages and salaries and the normal cash requirements of daily life. The bank rate was reduced from ten to six per cent.

Further change and more governmental control arrived with the

A troop of B Squadron of the Berkshire Yeomanry in Friar Street on the outbreak of the war. The soldier leading is Sergeant J.W. Cusden.

Before moving to its war station the yeomanry spent the first few days of the war in Reading, some stationed at the Queen's Hotel.

passing of what became known as DORA, the Defence of the Realm Act, on 8 August. 'It gave the government wide-ranging powers during the war period, such as the power to requisition buildings or land needed for the war effort, or to make regulations creating criminal offences.' It would have far-reaching effects and affect everyone. The Act was amended during the war, some aspects of it remained law well after the war was over, for example, pub opening hours during the day.

The war was barely three weeks old when this was taken. Caversham Laundry's annual outing on board the Britannia. *As the trip had been booked for months, it would have been a shame not to go even with a war on.*

The Act covered all aspects of life: 'no-one was allowed to talk about naval or military matters in public places; no-one was allowed to spread rumours about military matters; no-one was allowed to buy binoculars; no-one was allowed to trespass on railway lines or bridges; no-one was allowed to melt down gold or silver; no-one was allowed to light bonfires or fireworks; no-one was allowed to give bread to horses or chickens; no-one was allowed to use invisible ink when writing abroad; no-one was allowed to buy brandy or whisky in a railway refreshment room.' The government could take over land, factories and workshops, censor newspapers and prosecute civilians breaking the laws. The introduction of British Summer Time caused some issues but was generally seen as a positive measure on the other hand, restrictions on drinking raised far more objections: opening hours were cut, you could not buy a drink for someone else except with a meal – the no-treating regulation – and the beer was watered down. The first person to be arrested under DORA was the revolutionary socialist John MacLean, on 27 October 1915.

The harvest was collected despite the shortage of men and horses, but, according to local farmers, the crops were below average quality. Food prices started to rise, especially those of meat; this was put down to the fact that £5,000 worth of goods was being held at Hamburg. The government began to consider regulating retail grocery prices but fortunately there was an abundance of vegetables and fruit in the country. Even so, there was a rush on grocery shops. International Stores, the biggest grocers in the world, told Reading shoppers that their business was proceeding on a normal basis and that 'no prices advanced beyond what is enforced by market quotations; in many cases we are selling goods below market value.'

Livestock at the auction to raise funds for the National Relief Fund.

Everyone wanted to be involved, but only men of military age could help directly. The *Chronicle* provided 'A WORD TO THE PEOPLE' about how the civilian could assist the war effort. 'In the terrible times – yet only dimly realised – before us, English men and English women should practise the patriotism that consists not of shouting but in working for the common good. Civilians can do little positively to help their country, but they can refrain from doing the things that harm it. Among these are:-

1. Waste of every kind, especially of food and fuel. Petrol particularly should not be recklessly used.
2. Unnecessary harshness in demanding payment of debts during the period of financial stringency.
3. The selfish folly of withdrawing gold from the banks or hoarding up provisions, and all the fussiness and panic over money matters.
4. Embarrassing, by speech or act, those in authority.

Remember that in a great war like the present, the last sovereign counts as much as the last soldier.'

Another patriot offered advice for future mourners: 'In the course of the terrible war in which our country is now engaged many must undoubtedly be called upon to mourn the loss of one or more dear ones in the "fighting line", and unless something is done at the outset to discourage it a great deal of money which may later be needed to purchase the necessaries of life will be spent in buying "mourning clothes". May I suggest to all those who are thus bereaved that they

Posters outside the Town Hall proclaimed mobilisation.

should wear a simple mourning band, with a small crown stamped or embroidered on it, on the left arm instead of spending money on black clothes. No greater tribute could be paid to those who give their lives than the symbol that they did so for "King and country".'

Due to the war-caused shortage of newsprint, the mid-week edition of The *Chronicle* ceased to be published and the Friday edition was reduced. Readers were promised that, as soon as circumstances permitted, the number of pages would be restored. The Friday edition became the main paper; initially its main pre-occupation was sport and local affairs, which typically included deaths, stories from the courts, and reports of families doing their bit for the war effort. Among stories such as these were the tragic death of Mr Wabey, whose 14-year-old son accidentally blew off the top of his head and the whole of his brain in a shooting accident, and the eight members of one family called up for duty – James Bricknell's brothers, brothers-in-law and stepsons were all serving in the army. And there was what must be a Reading record: Charles Hamblin of Southampton Street's 61st conviction. He had been summoned for using obscene language on a corporation tram. During a rant in court, he told everyone that he was an Englishman, not a German, and that as long as he got justice they could do what they liked with him. He was willing to fight for King and Country as long as his convictions weren't put down, 'because the Kaiser wants one'. He was fined £1 plus costs or fourteen days in prison.

War news was limited to a request for old linen, flannel shirts and pyjamas for the troops and the Aliens Restriction Order issued by the County Borough. 'All German subjects residing in the Borough of Reading, who are not naturalised, must report themselves immediately at the Borough Police Station for registration.' The next week, there was a report of a gang of Germans occupying a house near Greyfriars Road; they turned out to be a peaceable family of Jews. Playing on the registration of aliens, the Palace Theatre ran a placard for its star turn: 'The loonies are one short: Has anyone seen the Kaiser?'

By the end of the month, fifty aliens had been registered in the

> Owing to the **WAR** the **MID-WEEKLY EDITION** of the 'CHRONICLE' will not be published unless special circumstances require it.

The paper shortage reduced both the frequency and page count of most newspapers.

borough. Two suspicious Germans were handed over to the military. Both were found to have military papers and one proved to be a deserter from the German Army. Later in the year, a German bookmaker, Richard Lawrence (Richard Schrenk), was found to be an unregistered enemy alien. Pretending to be Swiss, he had worked at regimental bases but had been taking note of what was happening under cover of his work. He was given six months' imprisonment because he was 'a source of real danger to the country'.

Concern over anything German extended beyond people. 'Dachshund dogs were put to sleep or attacked in the streets, a persecution which endured so long that in the years following the war the bloodline had to be replenished with foreign stock.' The reason for this hostility was simple: they symbolised Germany and were commonly used by political cartoonists to ridicule Germany. The phobia extended to food. Venner & Sons of Southampton Street, a well-known wholesale provision merchant, took the precaution of renaming one of their staple commodities, the German Sausage. It became the Empire Sausage. People with German names Anglicised them, including the Reading-born conductor of the Torquay Orchestra, Basil Hinderburg, who changed his name to Cameron to make sure that no-one was put off from attending his concerts.

Food prices continued to rise and people began to hoard food. International Stores explained the shortages in their stores. 'Last week the demand for goods on any one day equalled the usual demand for a week. It was entirely unnecessary and occasioned many difficulties that might have been avoided. In those instances where it led to disappointment to our customers we express our regrets.' As prices rose, quality sometimes fell short. Recurring themes in the Borough Police Court were underweight bread and poor quality milk. One case was that of Frederick King of 113 Elgar Road

FERGUSONS'

Anglo-Saxon

Beer.

IN BOTTLE :

BOTTLES.   ½-BOTTLES

2 6 per dozen.   1/6 per dozen.

IN CASK :

PIN.   FIRK.   KIL.

4 6   9 -   18 -

Telephone No. 80.

Brewed from British Malt and Hops for British People.

One way to show patriotism. Not that anyone would think that Fergusons' was a German name, the company were at pains to point out they would be drinking a purely British product.

who was summoned in October for selling milk which was not of the nature, substance and quality demanded, by reason of addition of water. He was fined £3 and costs.

The war also affected sporting fixtures. So many footballers of the Wednesday First Division had joined the colours that six clubs had resigned from the league. Henceforth there was no Wednesday football.

Like Britain, France called up its reservists, wherever they were living. Early on Wednesday, 19 August, 100 French Canadian reservists arrived in Reading on their way to Folkestone to cross the Channel. Having been escorted from Avonmouth by Thomas Cook representatives, they arrived in the GWR station just after noon and transferred to the South East and Chatham terminus to leave an hour later. News of their arrival quickly spread and soon the station yard thronged with citizens who enthusiastically greeted the visitors. 'As the time for the departure approached the French Canadians and citizens sang "God Save the King" and the "Marsellaise".' Responding to the cheers for both armies, the reservists waved the Tricolour and the Union Jack, as they pulled out of the station.

Recruiting was brisk and was widely reported. 'Reading is alive with troops, which are billeted in schools, public-houses, private residences and empty buildings.' At the barracks, recruitment for the New Army was 'going on apace at the barracks...every yard of

Youthful admirers watch the arrival of reservists.

Phyllis Dare recruitment evening in the Town Hall.

available ground is occupied by tents, each of them full of recruits.' Many came from the villages to enlist, others from afar because their local regiments were already full. A Hurst resident recalled many of his older compatriots going to Reading, some under-age but prepared to make a false statement so as not to miss out. Each of them received £1 from Captain Godsal at Haines Farm after enlisting.

There was a real pride in those who had gone to serve their country. How was this displayed? At a simple level this was clearly shown by the vicar of Sonning church. After Matins he 'would read out the names

A church parade of 8 Royal Berks and Army Service Corps men outside St. Giles' Church.

of men who had gone off to fight: William Cox, HMS *Excellent*, John Sumner, 1st Rifle Brigade, Arthur Edwards, Frederick White, Berkshire Yeomanry.'

We can tell from the following that children were just as caught up in the war as their parents. The children of St John's in Woodley wrote to their Sunday School teacher asking if they could help: 'We wondered if you were going to give us a Sunday School treat, but we think we could do without a treat this year, as so many soldiers are gone to war. Do you think we could spend part of the money in giving comforts to those who are gone from Woodley on active service? If so we would be so very pleased. SUNDAY SCHOOL SCHOLARS.'

King's Road Nursery.

We know of the pride of such villagers by their achievements. 'The ladies [of Sonning] reckoned that by the end of hostilities they had cut, sewed and folded 3800 yards of flannelette, 2230 of calico, 370 of khaki material for quilts and 500 of muslin for cap bandages and slings.'

With reservists being recalled and so many men volunteering, there was a rapid labour shortage that was felt by many of the town's employers, but at the same time there was also a reduction in orders.

Even with these problems, the *Reading Mercury* was able to report that Huntley & Palmers were going to look after their own: 'The great Reading Biscuit firm are showing every consideration possible for the well-being of their employees in this time of crisis, which is one that peculiarly affects their industry in many ways. The directors have taken, and will continue to take, steps to provide as much employment as is possible, and to help those dependent on them in every practicable manner.'

Huntley & Palmers were benevolent employers and gave freely to good causes throughout the war. They were able to be generous because they made large profits during the war. On 12 August the War Office gave the company substantial orders to manufacture army biscuits, which involved working continuously day and night for several weeks. In all over £84,000 worth of such orders were fulfilled to the end of March 1915 and £653,000 worth by November 1918, nearly 6½ per cent of total turnover. At the same time it was asked specially to pack 250,000 tons of basic rations provided by the government.

Among those joining the colours were two players from Reading Football Club, J. Dickenson (centre half) and Millership (back). Typical stories emphasised the patriotic attitude displayed by local villages and organisations and sometimes enlistments far away. Reading University College reported its pride in the numbers of men who had enlisted instead of starting the term (which was now to start on 1 October with a majority of female students). The local Dr Barnardo's could boast of thirteen lads who had volunteered and the band was helping the

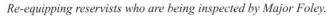

Re-equipping reservists who are being inspected by Major Foley.

recruiting drive in south London. Bracknell and local villages furnished a goodly number of recruits, with many giving up good jobs to do their duty. A newspaper report from further afield was that 8,000 French monks exiled in Spain had volunteered for service.

Men who joined the army in Reading but then left for camps elsewhere were replaced by men coming from other areas and regiments. Those breaking the law were not necessarily locals. Gunner Robert Gibson, of 30 Battery Royal Field Artillery, was sentenced to a month's hard labour for assaulting a ticket collector. He claimed that he was drunk but this was an inadequate excuse for a beating that left the collector crippled for some time.

With the British Army going into action came the realisation that there would be a need for assistance with the wounded. The Reading St John's Ambulance Association appealed for men with First Aid certificates to enrol with the brigade, something especially needed as thirty members had already enrolled with the RAMC.

At the same time, the Belgian Red Cross appealed for English nurses to help in Belgium. To aid the Belgians, Henley raised money for the Belgian Relief Fund

APPEAL
— BY —
J. Herbert Benyon, Esq.
(LORD LIEUTENANT OF THE COUNTY OF BERKSHIRE)
AND THE
Rt. Hon. Lord Haversham, P.C.
(CHAIRMAN OF THE BERKSHIRE TERRI- TORIAL FORCE COUNTY ASSOCIATION).

WE appeal to the men of Berkshire to offer themselves in large numbers for enlistment into the new Regular Army of 100,000 men which Lord Kitchener, as Secretary for War, has decided to form.

We feel sure it is only necessary to make it known throughout Berkshire that this new Army is necessary for every able-bodied man between the ages of 19 and 30 in the County to come forward and offer to enlist.

Ex-Soldiers under the age of 42 years (to whom precedence of joining will be given) may enlist to serve until they attain that age or until the end of the War. Ex-N.C.O.'s are particularly required to organise and train the new units.

The County of Berkshire has always hitherto proved itself ready and willing to offer its services for every patriotic movement, and we trust that many young men of this Royal County of Berkshire will come forward at the call of their King and Country.

A large Depôt is being formed at the Depôt, Royal Berkshire Regiment, Oxford Road, Reading, where all who wish to join can apply.

For the convenience of men in other towns and districts of the County, Recruiting Sergeants have been appointed, where applicants can obtain all information and Travelling Warrants for all those who may be selected.

The terms of enlistment are for a period of three years or for the period of the War as long as it lasts. Should the war be over in less than three years discharges can be obtained as soon as possible after the date it ceases.

Married men can be enlisted.

Below is a list of the places with the names of Recruiting Sergeants, where all information can be obtained.

J. HERBERT BENYON,
Lord Lieutenant of the County of Berkshire and President of the Berkshire County Association.

HAVERSHAM,
Chairman of the Berkshire County Association.

10th August, 1914.

The very small front page appeal by the Lord Lieutenant of Berkshire for volunteers to join the new army.

for the sick and wounded with the money going to the Ghent hospital authorities, while the Berkshire and South Oxon Adult School pledged to find temporary homes and hospitality for Belgian war refugees, women and children, now in this country and to raise a small weekly sum for the providing of homes for the refugees in the district. Thirty refugees arrived on 16 September to a hearty welcome. Most were

Nurses parading at King's meadow. The press thought that they were smarter than the men of the National Reserve.

Friendly and other societies paraded through Caversham and collected £67 for the Belgian Refugee Fund.

Mrs Haart, a Belgian refugee, who lived in Reading during the war.

Auction outside the Town Hall which raised £400 for the National Relief Fund.

women and children with a few men and boys. By mid-October, there were 200 Belgians in the Reading district and small parties continued to arrive.

It was obvious to the authorities that many families would need help for many different reasons and the Prince of Wales' National Relief Fund was set up. The Berkshire section of the fund was set up by the Lord Lieutenant, J.H. Benyon at Englefield House just outside Reading. He appealed for donations which would be acknowledged in the press. The Mayor of Reading sent out an appeal (in envelopes asking for donations) to nearly every house in Reading, delivered by volunteers. Collections were also set up by local firms and business houses. At the same time, a Prisoner of War Fund for the Berkshire Regiment was set up, which by 29 August, had collected £1,519-18s-5d.

It was soon realised that the fighting men would need more than was provided by the army or navy provided. The *Daily Mail* provided official patterns for knitted goods and Reading opened a Central Depot for the collection and distribution of suitable garments and other gifts for soldiers and sailors. These were to be sent to hospitals, the Red Cross and to the Berkshire Regiment.

The potential arrival of many wounded soldiers was a threat to the education of Reading's children. The army wanted to take over some schools as hospitals but Berkshire Council objected on the grounds that many private houses had been offered and would be just as suitable. However, the number of casualties grew rapidly and both private houses and schools were needed. The first Berkshire Regiment

Civilian driven Ford motor ambulances in Reading, provided by Messrs Skurray of Friar Street, for the Wellington Club, wait to be called to move the wounded.

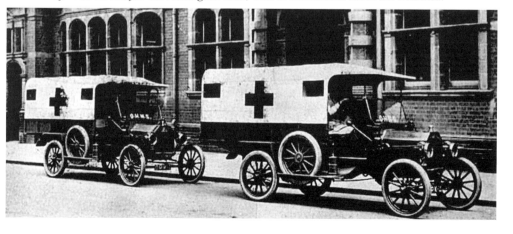

casualties appeared in the paper: Lieutenant T. Dennis (wounded) and Captain H. Shott and Major A. Scott-Turner (missing).

Numerous units arrived in the area for training and billeting. Many arrived at their war stations to guard vulnerable points, especially railway lines, and do jobs that would be taken over by volunteer units too old to serve at the front. Guarding gasworks, viaducts and bridges was straightforward but railway work was fraught with danger, particularly at night and in poor weather conditions. A number of lives were lost guarding the railway lines in and out of Reading.

A typical instance was reported in the 4 September edition of the *Chronicle*. The soldier guarding the main line from Maidenhead challenged a figure in the distance three times. Receiving no response he fired. Death was instantaneous. The deceased, a soldier from the unit, had climbed over the fence at the top of the embankment.

Visibility was also a key factor. Around the same time as the above, the paper reported the death of a cow: 'A Territorial on duty observed a white figure approaching. He gave the challenge "Halt, who goes there". He received no answer so he fired. Result, one dead cow!'

A few days later a soldier, no name reported, of 8 King's Regiment was run over by a train on the Reading to Basingstoke line. Private

A squad of King's Own Regiment guarding the GWR line near Reading.

A territorial battalion of the King's Own Regiment was tasked with guarding the GWR main line between Reading and Slough with out of date rifles.

Martindale of 4 King's Own was killed near Slough and Private Huartson of 5 King's Own died near Twyford. More deaths would follow before such patrols were handed over to local units. In the 16 October edition of the *Chronicle*, it was reported that railways would in future be guarded by the National Reserve in order to release regular and territorial soldiers.

It was not possible to provide sufficient guards or train them adequately for such dangerous employment. Before the scheme was dropped 'fourteen soldiers were killed by trains and two "own goals" were scored when nervous sentries shot dead the man coming to relieve them.'

National Reservists on King's Meadow.

Although life had changed, some things were constant. The papers still reported holiday travel in the United Kingdom, angling competitions and produce shows were still held, at one the winning marrow weighed in at thirty-one pounds and three and a half ounces.

The 11 September edition carried news of the first Reading casualty – Captain Buchanan-Dunlop of the West Kent Regiment was recovering from his wounds at home in Whitley Rise but was keeping himself busy speaking at recruiting meetings. The following week contained a list of men who had enlisted and what regiment they were joining. On a sadder note, it also contained the first of many Royal Berkshire Regiment and Oxford and Buckinghamshire Light Infantry casualty lists. While this was short, before too long it ran to half a page. The first reported deaths were two officers, Lieutenant Garnett (died of wounds) and Lieutenant Perrott (killed in action). Six privates were listed as wounded and recovering in UK hospitals: J.A. Bennett, G. Clarke, and H. Hamilton in the Alexandra Hospital at Cosham, F. Allen in the Connaught Hospital and G. Carter and A. Hainge in the Cambridge Hospital in Aldershot.

Able Seaman Harry Street of the Australian Naval and Military Expeditionary Force is buried in Rabaul War Cemetery in Papua New Guinea. He was killed in action on 11 September 1914 during the seizure of the German wireless station at Bitapaka. Why was he in a Reading paper? He was an Earley resident until he emigrated before the war.

Military fever was everywhere, even to 'the babes' as the *Mercury* reported. 'In one street in Reading the other evening a wide gateway was barricaded with big boxes, behind which youngsters with small guns took heavy toll of the passers-by. In some cases a wheelbarrow does duty for a Red Cross wagon, and sometimes you see a boy lying motionless on a sack borne by grave-faced schoolmates.'

Whether the story had been verified or not, atrocity letters were too good for a paper to pass up, especially when one came from a soldier in the local regiment. In the first months of the war came reports of German atrocities and activities that contravened the Geneva Convention. Private Goulding of the 1 Royal Berks Maxim detachment wrote about what he experienced. 'It was at two o'clock on a Sunday

Berkshire Red Cross ambulance workers working for the American Ladies Hospital in Torquay.

morning that we first saw the first German shell burst. Shortly after, five Belgian women came into our trenches. They were quite naked, and they were bleeding to death from wounds in the breasts, which, they said, the German officers had done with their swords. We did our best for the poor creatures, giving them our overcoats and jackets and bandaging them up as best we could. We then sent them under escort to our transport to be cared for. We counted fifteen Belgian women being pushed forward in front of the German firing line.'

It did not take long for a deserter to appear before Reading's magistrates. On 17 September, Private Frederick Sheppard of the Royal Warwickshire Regiment, appeared at the Police Court. Told that he could be shot for desertion he was detained for removal by the military authorities. The case was brief. He had enlisted on 12 September and deserted the next day because there was not enough food. He had been found at 6 Somerset Place.

The first local deaths appeared in the 25 September edition of the *Chronicle*: Lieutenant F. de Vere Bruce Allfrey (9th Lancers, killed in action near Provins) of Wokingham and Sergeant W. Murrell of Finchampstead. Lieutenant Allfrey, an only son, belonged to an important Wokingham family and on 21 September, two days before his birthday, a memorial service was held at All Saints Church in Wokingham. Following editions contained official and unofficial

Citizens of Reading wishing their best to the departing troops.

casualty lists. As the war progressed the lists became longer and more biographical.

In the same edition, a recruiting boom was reported: Royal Berks strength 8,600; 1,100 for the regular battalions; 2,000 for 3 Battalion; 1,500 for 4 Battalion; 1,100 for 5 Battalion; 1,100 for 6 Battalion and 500 in the depot unassigned. Even so the recruiting pressure continued: 'Young men are invited to join all branches of His Majesty's Army, free food, housing, clothing, pay, education and medical attendance provided. Tradesmen receive a high rate of pay in the RFC and the RE. Every opportunity is given to well-conducted men to obtain promotion.

Nottinghamshire Yeomanry detraining at Reading en route for further training on the Hardwick Estate at Whitchurch.

Well-educated men can obtain a commission as an officer after three years' service in the ranks, with a grant of £150 to purchase uniform, & £50 extra pay per annum for three years – further particulars apply by letter or personally to the Recruiting Officer, The Barracks, Reading.'

There was competition between the forces for recruits. Note the situations vacant columns of late September: 'Wanted, young men for the Royal Marines Artillery and Infantry, age 17 to 23, good pay, long service and pensions; also special, short service 3 years or for the duration of the war, age 19 to 30; stokers, age 18 to 25 – apply Colour Sergeant Nurse, 117 Cranbury Road, Reading.'

The whole nation was caught in the spy scare with many peaceful British citizens being accused of being German or spying for Germany. Reading photographer Marcus Adams, while waiting for the train to Reading, sat on a canal bank to sketch White Horse Hill. Two

COMMISSIONS IN THE REGULAR ARMY, SPECIAL RESERVE & TERRITORIAL FORCE.

Gentlemen resident in Reading and neighbourhood desirous of obtaining Commissions are invited to apply, either personally or by letter, to

The Officer Commanding,
Officers Training Corps,
University College, Reading.

For those wishing to obtain a commission, University College ran an Officers Training Corps, so it was natural that they initially be in charge of selection.

2nd South Midland Mounted Brigade.

CHAUFFEURS, ENGINEERS, FITTERS, SMITHS, etc. Recruits wanted for Mechanical Transport Company Army Service Corps. To join for four years or period of war.

Recruits also required for Horse Transport Company. DRIVERS, ARTIFICERS, BUTCHERS, BAKERS, FARRIERS, WHEELERS, SADDLERS, etc. Good opportunity for Ex-Army Service Corps N.C.O.'s and men desirous of again serving.

For full particulars as to rates of pay, etc., apply Recruiting Officer, Army Service Corps, Yeomanry House, Reading.

Why join the infantry when the rates of pay were much higher if you had a trade the army needed?

boys walked up and whispered: 'Look there's a German.' Rapidly a crowd formed. Under many watchful eyes, he packed up, threw his camera over his shoulder and walked towards the station. Having been stopped by a policeman who would not believe his account, he had to show his passport and the crowd had to be assured he was not a spy before he could continue. However, it was reported in the 12 September edition that three spies had been arrested in Reading, Johannes Ramm, Edward Beckman and Gustav Paul. They were handed over to the military. What happened to them is not known other than they were not shot.

Were there really spies, and, as they were called twenty-five years later, fifth columnists all over Berkshire? Did the public really think they were everywhere? It would appear most people assumed so. At Basildon on 22 August a sentry in the vicinity of Gatehampton Railway Bridge saw two men in a meadow near the bridge and fired two rounds at them. Proceeding to where he saw the men he was fired at. He returned fire and searched the locality but found nothing. In total eight shots were fired. Thames Conservancy men on duty heard shots but saw no one.

Was it the reward they were after? Where there were no potential spies it was possible to invent them. In late September Josiah Hawkins, deemed a lunatic, was detained for wandering in Queen Victoria Street. He told the arresting Police Constable that he had found a German and wanted the £1000 reward for his arrest. He claimed besides that he had bought up all the free public houses in England. As he could not say where he lived, he was taken to the Poor Law Institution. 'The prisoner said he was about to take the Falcon at Theale when he saw a stranger, who could not speak English, and marched him into Reading, where he let him go, as he had no firearms. The German kissed him and they parted quite friends.' Dr Guilding, the Institution Medical Officer, said he evidently suffered from delusions, and although calm and quiet, was obviously not of sound mind. Shortly after this incident, the Berkshire County Asylum invited suppliers to submit tenders and samples in quart bottles, to provide beer and ale for the inmates. Was this to calm them down?

While reporting that 'so many German spies are now in the country (that) the strictest watch is being kept at all the military departments in and around Reading,' the *Chronicle* focussed on many local stories as well as finding space for more important events such as the sinking of the *Aboukir*. The court cases at the start of the war differed little from those before or during; the war brought about no reduction in the work of the courts.

Herewith some typical cases. Two twenty-three-year-olds were convicted of playing pitch and toss on Jubilee Square and fined 2s 6d plus costs. A farm labourer was fined 10s in absentia for obscene language; he told the court he couldn't afford to miss a day at work. Jane Simpson in Warfield was found guilty of being drunk and disorderly outside her house where she was making a disturbance and challenged PC Nicholls to a fight. The magistrate bound her over on £2 to be of good behaviour for twelve months, advising her to take the pledge. Four Reading children, aged between 9 and 13, pleaded guilty to committing damage to a barrel of beer and doing injury to the amount of 10s. They had removed a cork from the barrel and wasted ten gallons of beer; then one gave a false name and address. They were discharged with a severe caution and their parents were bound over for their good behaviour for twelve months to the sum of £3. The magistrate told the court that 'out of pure mischief and wantonness the lads had accomplished a great deal of damage and done serious injury to other people'. Alfred Bilson was charged and convicted with an indecent assault on a 9-year-old girl in the recreation ground in Tilehurst. Admitting 'it was the drink that made him feel funny', he pleaded guilty with no recollection of what had occurred. His eight previous convictions for similar offences were taken into account and he was sentenced to six months' hard labour.

At first, actions on the Western Front took second place to the happenings on the Home Front, though quickly lengthy articles about the daring deeds of the Berkshire Regiment did appear. A recurrent theme in the Magistrates Court throughout the war was desertion. Most gave themselves up, like Private Harry East of the Welsh Regiment. After a few days' freedom, he confessed on 23 September, was charged the next day and handed back to the military. A taxi driver was fined for negligent driving, cricket scores were reported and visits to Suttons Seeds noted. Money lenders advertised rock bottom rates and shipping lines promoted travel to North America. The Royal Berkshire Hospital recorded its activity: forty-one patients admitted, thirty-eight discharged and thirty-five operations.

A Belgian wedding held in Reading.

Important marriages were dutifully recorded, many with a complete listing of the gifts received. With a war on, many toned down the celebration. 'The marriage arranged between the Hon. Gerald Rufus Isaacs, only son of the Lord Chief Justice of England and Lady Reading, and Eva, eldest daughter of the Right Hon. Sir Alfred Mond, Bart., P.C., M.P., and the Lady Mond, will take place on Monday next. The wedding will be quiet, and only immediate relations will be present.'

Economy extended to business as well. Employees at Suttons benefited from the company's drive to save electricity, while at the same time maintaining full employment, at full-time on full pay. From 30 October, the hours of work were 8.30 am to 1 pm and 2.15 pm to 5 pm.

Across the country men volunteered for a wide range of reasons. Some did not want to miss the adventure; for others it was an escape from a humdrum existence; some were patriotic; some followed their friends. The reasons were myriad. John Stevens, from Brimpton, twelve miles south-west of Reading, asked to be allowed to volunteer to expunge his crime. He was charged with stealing a parcel he was supposed to post. The magistrate adjourned the case for a month during which time he enlisted. He survived the war.

Even with the severe manpower shortage and a lowering of physical standards, not all who volunteered were taken. Most who were rejected took it in their stride and accepted it and others attempted to do something about it. One failed volunteer spent six weeks exercising and improved his health and strength sufficiently to be accepted. Some though could not forgive. One man, turned down twice because of a rupture, got his revenge by setting fire to a hayrick that had been bought by the government. He was caught and admitted the offence. Another Berkshire man gave false information about his hip and managed to pass the medical. Unable to cope with the training he was discharged from the service and given one month's imprisonment with hard labour (a reduced sentence because he had a wife and three children). His crime: wasting time and costing the country money.

Many of those who were unable, through age or ill-health, to join the regular forces, decided to do their bit for the defence of the realm. By mid-October, the Reading Citizen Army was able to boast 700 members, mostly business men. Reading's athletes formed their own

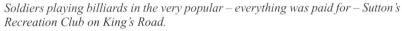

Soldiers playing billiards in the very popular – everything was paid for – Sutton's Recreation Club on King's Road.

army, the Athletes Volunteer Force. They had a membership of over 200 men. Both were part of the Reading Citizens Defence Force.

There was no shortage of men willing to join the Volunteer Force. The Earley and District Defence had risen to seventy-one members with five service rifles between them. The Reverend Wardley-King provided them with thirty carbines and Mr Joel, its president, agreed to provide land for a rifle range. In Reading, the Athletes' Force had reached a membership of 550.

While the irregular forces were experiencing no shortage of recruits, the regulars, territorials and New Army were still advertising for men. The 4th (HS) Battalion advertised for men between the ages of 18¾ and 35 and NCOs up to 50. Every recruit was expected to undertake liability for general service at home and abroad if required.

Alderman C G Field was the Mayor of Reading when the war broke out.

The mayor went on record to commend the men of Reading for their patriotism, telling a recruiting meeting that Reading was held in the highest esteem throughout the kingdom, especially in the south of England. He declared that Reading had taken a lead before all districts as a recruiting place, and noted that in proportion to the population they stood above other towns in the number of men recruited. By the end of October, the Reading Roll of Honour was over 4,000 men.

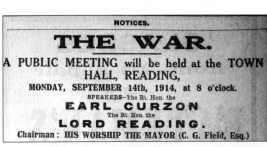

NOTICES.

THE WAR.

A PUBLIC MEETING will be held at the TOWN HALL, READING,

MONDAY, SEPTEMBER 14th, 1914, at 8 o'clock.

SPEAKERS—The Rt. Hon. the

EARL CURZON

The Rt. Hon. the

LORD READING.

Chairman: HIS WORSHIP THE MAYOR (C. G. Field, Esq.)

An advert from the Reading Standard. *At the time, Lord Curzon was travelling the United Kingdom delivering speeches explaining the war and encouraging men to enlist.*

Lord Curzon speaking in the small Town Hall. At the table are Alderman Field, Sir Percy Sanderson and Lord Reading.

Lord Curzon's view of the meeting – a packed hall.

Football teams were fertile grounds for recruitment. Many news snippets concerned player enlistment and the reduced number of teams in a league. Earley F.C. reported at the end of September that sixteen of their members had joined up: three had joined the local Territorial Horse Artillery, three or four were in Kitchener's Army and the remainder were in the Berkshire Territorials.

Department stores angled their sales to suit the times. A Heelas department store advertisement fitted the prevailing military mood: '3000 full size khaki Army blankets in stock at 7s 9d each. Sound and hard wearing to the last shred and distinctly not a blanket that is all fluff. 5s for defective brown army blankets – body warmers. Acceptable gift to all ranks of our soldiers, a soft-finished shrunk wool under vest with long sleeves, 5000 in stock at 3s, not the usual 3s 6d.'

Throughout the war many organisations asked for donations. The Berkshire Regiment Tobacco Fund was one of the first with its appeal to the smokers of Berkshire: 'from their homes and dear ones, fighting night and day against terrible odds, waist deep in water as they crouch in the shell-swept trenches, at least 800 Berkshire smokers are giving

Fund raising gave a purpose to many. The boys on the right have their boxes ready.

limbs and lives for you. Will you do something for them? Will you keep their pipes filled? Smokers know the priceless value of that boon. Hunger, cold, exposure, fatigue and danger can all be mitigated by the soldier's pipe. See that at least they have that.' The '*Weekly Dispatch*' agreed to forward the tobacco on but £120 was needed to provide tobacco until the end of the year. 'We appeal to all smokers. You Sir, enjoying your Corona after dinner, send the price of a box…You ladies, sampling a Vafiadis [an Egyptian cigarette] with your dearest friend in your own den, think of the gallant lad wistfully regarding his empty pipe; start a collection for our fund, and do it quickly.'

Flag and badge days became a part of life during the war. Belgian Favours Day on Saturday, 26 September was one of many fund-raising events in the first year of the war. Large numbers

Young flag sellers on one of the first Red Cross days of the war.

of volunteers were needed for a successful event. Between 700 and 750 ladies were out selling the favours for the day, with 200 collecting

After eleven hours of selling favours, £551 was raised to help Belgian refugees.

boxes, and raised £551 5s 9d by selling 80,000 paper badges. Not all appeals for funds were for the fighting man. The first Blue Cross day on 7 November raised £430 to care for sick and wounded horses at the front.

Not all appeals were local. Like other towns, Reading responded to a national appeal for the troops. To supplement War Office stocks before winter, Lord Kitchener asked the Queen to provide 300,000 knitted or woven belts and 300,000 pairs of socks by early in November for immediate distribution to the front. The Queen gave her assent and asked the women of the Empire to assist her. Reading's women began to knit, and did not stop until the war ended.

Many women and girls wanted to help in any way they could. In November, the Town Hall was filled by an enthusiastic audience of girls who had answered to the call, 'Come and hear how you can help your country in this time of war.' They were urged to join the League of Honour which banded together women and girls across the Empire in doing their bit to help their country and the men who fought its battles on land and sea. The League's members took an individual pledge: 'I promise, by the help of God, to do all that is in my power to uphold the honour of our nation and its defenders in this time of war, by prayer, purity, and temperance.'

The next month saw the formation of the Reading Women's Volunteer Corps, an offshoot of London's Women's Volunteer Reserve.

Making bedding and pillowcases for the army somewhere in Reading.

They were not 'a fierce band of women, going about shooting and doing everything masculine'; their purpose was general utility and competence. To that end they were 'taught signalling, telegraphy, nursing, cooking, first aid and other things'. Whilst they felt they should be armed and taught how to shoot, they knew that they would have to wait for the order. Their motto was 'mens sana in corpore sano' – inspiring them with a 'goal well worth kicking'.

It is not often that drinking too much can contribute to your survival. However, an excess of alcohol, taken on leave by Private Garlick, meant that he missed the 1914 battles in which his battalion suffered heavily. When the 2nd Battalion docked at Liverpool, it moved to Hursley Park to re-fit. Before moving to France, the division was given forty-eight hours leave. The men went home to say their goodbyes or, in the case of one Berkshire soldier, to drink. Private Garlick spent the entire leave 'elevated'. In such an 'elevated' condition he and his cousin attempted to cycle to visit a relative. He hit a rut, fell, and injured his elbow. Somehow his relatives got him on a train to Winchester where he hitched a lift. The driver of the vehicle threw him out just before the guardroom and he fell asleep in a ditch. After parade, minus his puttees, he was sent to hospital where his elbow was operated on. He did not return to his battalion until January 1915.

On the same day as the 2nd Battalion docked, the 41st annual report of the Medical Officer for Reading was published, reflecting the constantly improving health of the borough. During 1914 infantile mortality and the death rate were low and there had been little infectious disease; diphtheria, typhoid fever and measles cases were much below the average. The one case of smallpox was blamed on another town. The population was growing: 1066 died and 1861 were born (985 males and 876 females), with a net death rate of 11.58 per 1000 of population and a net birth rate of 20.94. Reading's population was also living longer. The death rate was broken down: 150 deaths under one year old, thirty-seven between one and five, 467 between five and sixty-five, 380 at sixty-five or older, with one female of unknown age who had drowned. In the last age group, fifty-six men and seventy-five women had 'survived the eightieth year of their lives, of whom ten, three men and seven women, lived to ninety and upwards. The oldest person was a female who had attained the age of 103.' The oldest male was ninety-one. Overall the death rate for men was higher:

St Luke's Parish Hall on Erleigh Road was converted into a Red Cross Hospital by 34th Berks VAD.

12.72 per thousand with women at 10.96. Infant mortality was still high with a death rate for under one year of age at 80.2 per thousand.

While the 2nd Battalion had been returning from India, the 1st Battalion was fighting on the Aisne. As many Reading men were now fighting, the *Chronicle* started printing letters and diary extracts, many quite detailed. It reported the extent of injuries, prisoners, and information on deaths. Readers were told of Signaller George Henry Lee of 3 Essex Street, who was recovering in Connaught Hospital, Aldershot, from shrapnel in the back that nearly paralysed him for life; and Reading taxi driver, Dan Robertson, who died saving his wounded sergeant, and Reading's first prisoner of war, Lieutenant Henderson, the son of the Chief Constable of Reading, who was unwounded, in good health and fairly comfortable in the PoW camp at Torgau.

Initially, military censorship was light and many men wrote home describing both their experiences and whereabouts. Later letters still described their doings, but places were not mentioned. A typical early letter was sent by Private Maurice Hawkins, serving with the Royal Naval Division. Writing from Ostend he told his parents: 'You will be surprised to hear that I was in the siege of Antwerp, and a rough time we had too. We had our trenches shelled for seventy-two hours. Several got killed, but I was lucky and got away…I have a bit of shell that hit me on my hat.'

Some families became minor celebrities, with their photos appearing in the papers, because of the number of sons serving with the colours. Some were even notified that the king knew about them. One such letter, to the Taylors, a Slough family, is mentioned in the *Chronicle*, although there were Reading families who equalled the number of sons serving. The Keeper of the Privy Purse wrote: 'I have the honour to inform you that the King has heard with much interest that you have six sons serving in the Army. I am commanded to express to you the King's congratulations, and to assure you that His Majesty much appreciates the spirit of patriotism which prompted this example in one family of loyalty and devotion to their Sovereign and Empire.' Whether Mr Walley of 13 Derby Street received a letter the paper did not specify. He should have, as he also had six sons serving and a seventh, Arthur, a Corporal in 1 Royal Berkshire Regiment, who had served in the Boer War, and who had been invalided home. His other two sons, not currently in the army, had fought in the Boer War.

The initial enthusiasm for recruitment waned. To find out who might be persuaded to enlist, it was decided to produce a register of

The Hunt family of Twyford had five men in the forces.

GEO. HUNT, Royal Flying Corps.

ALFRED HUNT, H.M.S. Minotaur.

ARTHUR HUNT, 3rd Batt. Royal Berks Regiment.

The late ALBERT EDWARD HUNT, who was lost with Submarine E3.

JOHN HUNT, Northumberland Fusiliers.

A card provided to households where a member was serving with the colours.

With six sons serving in the army in the first weeks of the war was the proud record of Mr and Mrs Slade of 35 Katesgrove Lane who received a letter of congratulation from the King. Although named in the original, who they are is not indicated. Which photo matches the names was not indicated in the original but they are: Private Francis, ex 1st Royal Berks - disqualified through ill-health (centre top); Private W A, who served in the South African War and who was then in the Canadian Army (bottom right); Private Ernest, who had previously served in India (top right); Private Reginald, who was serving with the Ox & Bucks Light Infantry (top left); Private A E, serving with the 5th Royal Berks (bottom left) and Sergeant A, who fought in the South African War and was training men at Brock Barracks (bottom centre).

"I am commanded by the King to convey to you an expression of his Majesty's appreciation of the patriotic spirit which has prompted you and your five sons to give their services at the present time to his Majesty's Forces.

"The King was much gratified to hear of the manner in which they have so readily responded to the call of their Sovereign and their country, and I am to express to you and to them his Majesty's congratulations on having contributed in so full a measure to the great cause for which all the people of the British Empire are so bravely fighting."

The King's message to Mr Byrne.

those willing to enlist at some time. Every householder in Reading, part of the Army's Southern Command, received a letter from the Parliamentary Recruiting Committee on behalf of the War Office. With the letter was a form asking for the names and other particulars of men, between the ages of nineteen and thirty-eight, residing in the house, who were willing to enlist for the duration only. The names were to be placed in a register, allowing the nearest recruiting officer to arrange to attest those required when their services were required.

A Situations Vacant advert demonstrated the need by both services for men: 'Men wanted for the Royal Navy, Royal Marines and the Royal Naval Division. Height from 5′ 2″, horse drivers, age 19 to 38, farriers, wheelers, saddlers, age 19 to 45. Pay at army rate. Allowances at navy rate.' However, by this time, Reading was able to boast a Roll of Honour of over 4,000 enlistments.

One important question was hotly debated: in view of the war, and with many horses being taken by the army, should fox hunting continue? The Berkshire Hunts decided that it should, and for very good reasons: 'Any stoppage will cause unemployment, and it should be continued as long as needed in order to kill as many foxes as necessary in the country,' but this would not be done as sport until the war was over. The same decision was reached on the other side of the

Mrs Buckett of 1 Limehouse Court, had six sons serving. Although named on the original photograph, they are not identified. The only recognisable son is centre standing: Colour Sergeant Archibald, a drill instructor on Salisbury Plain.

Thames in Oxfordshire: 'The South Oxfordshire Hounds will meet on Monday, November 9th at Wheatley Bridge; on Wednesday November 11th at Horsepath; and on Friday, November 13th at Waterperry Common.' In the same vein, the GWR announced excursions to watch the races at Warwick and a whole range of day trips that were available.

At the same time as it was reporting the local Hunt Meetings, the feature leader writer of the *Chronicle* was telling readers how well the war was going for the Allies. The Russians were pushing the Austro-German forces out of Poland, and the British, French and Belgians were more than holding their own. The 'Contemptible Little Army' was 'bearing the brunt of an assault by overwhelming German forces, but they have held their ground with tenacity, and inflicted heavy losses on their enemy.'

Belgian Refugee Day. Vendors selling Belgian favours to raise money to help Reading's newest inhabitants.

What the writer did not mention was that the Germans were themselves inflicting heavy casualties on the British Army. Reading found this out on 3 November when the first wounded arrived at the Royal Berks Hospital from Oxford. The freshly-bandaged men who had all been wounded by shell and shot arrived at Reading station just before midday, where they were met by volunteers driving their own cars and a new ambulance bought by the Wellington Club.

This was the start of Reading becoming a hospital town with

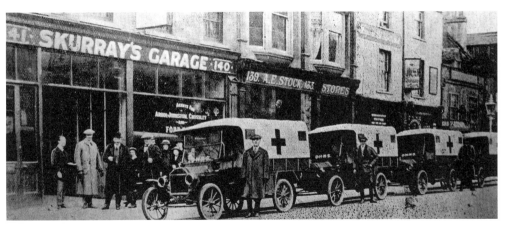

Ford motor ambulances outside Skurray's garage on Friar Street.

The 13th Berks VAD at Reading Railway Station. The patients were conveyed to the local war hospitals by the Berkshire Voluntary Aid Transport Service organised by the Berkshire Automobile Club. Motorists lent their cars which were then converted and the general public subscribed to buy ambulances.

schools, large private houses and other buildings being converted into military hospitals. Typical examples were Englefield House, home of the Benyon family, and Beenham Valance, home of Sir Richard Sutton. The Lord Lieutenant provided a wing of his stately home for recovering wounded and the 'long gallery' was fitted out as a hospital with twenty beds. Both owners also paid all the expenses.

Red Cross volunteers of 13th Berks VAD being inspected by the mayor of Reading in October 1914.

Struan House VAD Hospital for convalescents decorated for Christmas.

Along with the VAD-operated house hospitals, Reading by 1916 had six War Hospitals. The Reading War Hospital on Oxford Road opened on 22 April 1915; No. 2 War Hospital (Battle School) opened on 1 July 1915; No. 3 War Hospital (Wilson School) opened on 7 September 1915; No. 4 War Hospital (Redlands School) opened on 25 June 1915; No. 5 War Hospital (Katesgrove School) opened after March 1916.

Passing time whilst recovering. Wounded soldiers playing cards in the summer sun.

Swift and comfortable travel for the wounded. Ambulances at Reading War Hospital with drivers ready for the next ambulance train to arrive at the station.

As the war 'that would be over by Christmas' moved towards its first December, more articles appeared about local men, the local regiment, their gallant fighting, stories of brave deeds and information about individuals. The following are typical stories about Reading men in the trenches: 'Sergeant A. Cripps of 21 Warren Place has been commended for bravery and Mentioned in Dispatches. He swam across a river and rescued an officer from a storm of bullets from a bridge. He was badly wounded in the arm, but got his man back to the lines safely. He worked in the saw mill at Huntley & Palmers before he was called from the reserve. He is anxious to get back to the trenches.' Private W.H. Albones of 3 Coldstream Guards spent his birthday, 1 November, in the trenches. The next day he was wounded in both legs. In the terrible fighting that day 'there were hundreds of us caught by shot or shell, and a good many, unfortunately, were killed; but for all that we were thinning the Germans out a bit.' Rifleman Joseph Hunt from Reading, serving with the Rifle Brigade, was reported to be a PoW. He had been shot through the wrist, broken his arm and eventually been brought down by a bullet through the ankle. He wrote that he had nothing whatever to complain of in respect of the treatment meted out to him. And of course there is the lucky escape story. Sergeant J.C. Seward, a reservist in the Royal West Kents, who worked in Reading, wanted another crack at the Germans after what they did to him. 'A big shell burst in our trench, and two men and myself were completely buried by the sides of the trench being blown in. It was an awful feeling being buried alive and slowly suffocating. Our chaps dug us out, thank God!'

The dining hall at Maitland Road Red Cross Hospital which cared for soldiers who fell sick during training and convalescents. It was organised and staffed by 52 Berks VAD.

D Company of 8 Royal Berks burying a comrade.

As the casualties rose, many felt that the government owed gratitude to the fighting man. At a local meeting, the Secretary of the National Union of Railwaymen said: 'now was the time to insist that the Government provided pensions of not less than £1 per week for soldiers, marines or sailors who were totally disabled as a result of the war and for the widows of those killed.'

Not all military deaths were the result of enemy activity. Some died of disease, some in tragic accidents, others took their own lives. Private Robert Evans, who had enlisted on 3 September in 7 Royal Berks Regiment, died of gas asphyxiation in Friar Street YMCA. Private Julius Mycock of 22 Vachel Road was serving with the Hampshire Isle of Wight National Reserve guarding railway lines when he was found with his throat cut. His suicide was put down to his debts.

A number of public houses had closed since the start of the war because magistrates had failed to renew licences, some because they were unsavoury, others because of their proximity to places of manufacture when war production required a sober workforce. In November it was proposed to regulate opening hours. The decision was to close at 10 pm in the borough and 9 pm in the county. This was to apply to clubs as well and was to come into operation on 9 November. This change to normal life was not popular.

Casualties and DORA did not dampen the need to look respectable, and, for department stores like Heelas, it was business as usual in November with the Christmas period ahead. Fashion goods were still available with Heelas 'selling a number of the finest original model creations of the great houses of Paris. Each and every one of the gowns shown was purchased as an original creation in Paris, and still bears the name ticket of the designer – names famous in the World of Fashion', for example a model gown by Marcel Kahn that was originally 8 guineas was down to 3. A smart gown by Gouget and Lorimer was similarly priced.

Heelas reminded their customers that Christmas was coming and that they would prepare for a normal festive season: 'Our Christmas Bazaar has now become so much a feature of Christmas to boys and girls that in order not to disappoint them we have decided to hold it this year "as usual" and it will open on SATURDAY, the 21st inst (21 November). There will be a shooting range and a Skittle Alley with the Kaiser all ready to be knocked over.'

The theme of Christmas was continued by the mayor. Next to articles on Madame Clara Butt's concert, greyhound racing, and a list of 1 Royal Berks casualties, he appealed, as usual, for money. This time it was to buy Christmas puddings for the Royal Berkshire Regiment men who were fighting with Rawlinson's IV Corps. His wife needed £800 for 4000 puddings for everyone in the corps. Pledging £5, the mayor invited readers to contribute to the fund. This coincided with a scheme to raise further money for the National Relief Fund. Princess Mary's Gift Book was on sale in an edition of 250,000, with all profits going to the fund.

The start of the cold weather gave William McIlroy Ltd a reason to

With colder weather approaching came another way to sell goods.

Reading Trade and Friendly Societies' Parade in aid of The Prince of Wales' Fund raised £137.

encourage customers to feel part of the war: 'For that boy or friend at the front, 7/6 d parcel usually 8/0½d. 1 pair warm gloves, 1 Woollen body belt, 1 pair woollen socks, sleeping cap, khaki braces, beautiful wool scarf.'

What happened to all the aliens previously mentioned and why had this step been taken? Twenty miles west of Reading, a concentration camp for some 600 aliens was set up at Newbury Racecourse. They came from all over the country and were housed in the stables. By November, the camp housed 3,000, with new arrivals arriving regularly. The local papers described them as the 'enemy in our midst', removed so they were 'out of harm's way to safeguard against espionage'. In the local round-up of Austrians and Germans aged between seventeen and fifty were waiters and tailors and a well-known publican, Max Seeburg who had played for Reading F.C. professionally until 1913.

They were initially guarded by Territorials, but later came under the jurisdiction of the Berkshire National Reserve. The internees had their own money for purchases from local suppliers. As the railways were still running cheap travel, the camp became a minor attraction. 'The internees duly entertained their audience with pick-a-back races, flat races for prizes of cigarettes, danced the tango to mouth organ music and held nightly camp concerts.' It did not always run smoothly and, after complaints by the prisoners, the camp was investigated (for poor accommodation and food) by the American State Department (a neutral power that protected Germans who were imprisoned in Britain). Before its closure it is thought to have held well over a thousand internees as well as a further 1,000 prisoners of war in tents elsewhere on the course.

Although the Police Report in 1915 would show a fall in criminal offences, the courts continued to be busy with the usual pre-war crimes. Cautioning drovers for contravening a bye-law against driving bullocks up the Wokingham Road to Earley Station on a Sunday morning; sending a 15-year-old boy to Reformatory School for three years for setting fire to two haystacks; committing a 10-year-old boy to an unspecified stay in the North London Industrial School in Walthamstow for stealing two tins of salmon valued at 1s 9d; and remanding Herbert Mills, a man of feeble mind, from Orts Road, who was convicted of impropriety, in order to send him to an institution. They also granted Rhoda Emily Squires of Great Knollys Street a separation order from her husband Alfred who was ordered to pay 5s a week to her, and granted her custody of the younger children. She had filed on the grounds of persistent cruelty. Pleading tearfully for mercy, Alfred admitted the truth of the complaint. During their fifteen-year marriage he had often blackened her eyes, once even on their wedding day, had frequently left her and also threatened to be the death of her. As there were still no restrictions on purchasing petrol, car drivers continued to cause problems, but the laws on drink driving were lax and many were able to get off. George Emmett of 24 Whitley Street was charged with being drunk in charge of a motor car. He told the magistrates that he had only had four or five glasses of beer and was perfectly sober. All in the car agreed they were all sober. The summons was dismissed because of doubt about his condition.

With many policemen recalled to the colours, it was necessary to enlist men unable to serve in the forces as Special Constables. Unmarried men between nineteen and thirty-nine were eligible to serve, if circumstances made it impossible for them to join the forces. Single men aged seventeen to nineteen could serve until they reached recruitment age. Each man was provided with a baton and 'wore a blue and white armlet that held the word "special".' Their main function was to prevent disorder, but in Wokingham they were tasked with guarding the Post Office, the gasworks, the waterworks and the railway bridges.

Service in the 'specials' ran through the social classes. One well-connected member was the Marquis of Downshire at Easthampstead Park. He chauffeured his own car as part of his detachment's resources. How the public felt about their usefulness is shown by two jokes in the *Chronicle*. 'One of Reading's Constables was confronted with an awkward situation the other evening. A woman rushed out of a house with blood flowing from a wound in her throat. "I'll make a report of it," he calmly said, and walked on.' 'The other evening a woman came running up to a Special Constable in Reading. "Do come, there are two men fighting, and they will kill one another." The 'Special' looked at her, and remarked, "What you want is a proper policeman – one in uniform".'

During the first months of the war, the loss of tradesmen to the forces made itself felt. Getting workmen became a major task, but also gave those tradesmen still working more business and the chance to charge higher prices. Other avenues of employment were being opened by the war, but the reduction in income felt by many meant they could no longer afford to have servants. While some took over jobs vacated by troops, some took another option – emigration. The demand for British domestic servants was high in Canada, and assisted by the Salvation Army, many went to guaranteed employment there.

By December, 515 Huntley & Palmers employees were with the colours. As good employers they had guaranteed both jobs for returning servicemen and adequate provision for their families while they were away.

The 4 December issue of the *Chronicle* contained a detailed casualty list. Now the populace would know who had been killed, died, died of wounds or wounded and which hospital they were in, some with details of their wounds, injuries or condition provided: Private C. Priest in Boulogne hospital had a hernia and Private E.W. Woodman was suffering from contusion. This level of detail did not survive long; reports soon concentrated on the basic details and where the soldiers came from.

In the same issue, retailers' thoughts turned to Christmas sales. Messrs Hickie & Hickie told readers they had a large stock of new and

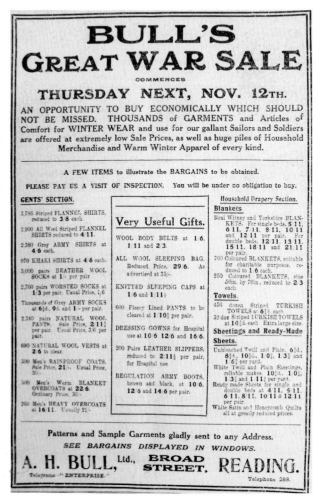

One of many adverts that would use the war to help move goods. The Bull's of Broad Street Great War Sale provided residents with necessities for their loved ones serving in the forces.

second-hand pianofortes, from seven guineas upwards, and American organs and harmoniums. They also had a selection of first-class gramophones and a stock of over 2,000 records. Messrs Millwards & Sons had a great variety of comfortable and useful slippers available at prices to suit all pockets. Hedgecocks in Broad Street were offering high class Christmas and New Year's gifts: dainty hankies, fans, lace

Christmas dinner for 8 Royal Berks was held in Vincent's garage on Castle Street.

goods, silk blouses for the ladies, and mitts, socks, helmets, scarves and shirts for the men.

A festive season requires food and decorations. Mr Grant of 58 Oxford Street, Caversham was selling a special line of oranges at thirty for 1s. He was also able to provide decorations to complete the festive home: holly and mistletoe. At 63 Oxford Road and 106 King's Road, Mr T. Mason had a fine selection of English turkeys, geese, ducks and fowl from which to choose for Christmas dinner.

Although many were struggling financially, people sent Christmas cards in their thousands. The *Chronicle* explained that it was almost a patriotic thing to send them as this provided work for thousands of people. Business as usual was hoped for as people placed orders for private cards with their stationer or newsagent. With a war on, it was obvious to publishers that there would be a need for patriotic messages such as 'God speed our forces on land and sea, in defence of freedom and right, May our victories bring us lasting peace.' For those who had lost a loved one, it would not be a joyous season but there was still a need to send cards. These were usually simple in design and embossed in black with a black ribbon.

Fund raising was constant throughout the war, and ever more novel ways of raising money were invented. At the Henley Christmas market, a cigar was auctioned – not just any old cigar, but one given to a

A typical patriotic card from the first war Christmas.

A Christmas card sent by William Hubbard of Richmond Street, Reading who was in mourning. The ribbon and the motif are black and the card is edged in grey.

Hambledon resident by Lord Lonsdale, who had been given it by the Kaiser. The cigar was sold and re-sold and raised £14 10s for the local Red Cross hospital.

Presumably as a Christmas present, Reading Parks Department changed their minds and decided to allow troops to use Prospect and Palmer parks for military exercises and the Reading Volunteers Forces to drill in Palmer Park. It was also decided by the council that troops could use swimming pools free of charge and that Hills, Tilehurst Road and King's Meadow pools were to be exclusively for troops.

The mayor of Reading buying a Belgian favour.

Some of the reservists called at the start of the war had been well-prepared for such an eventuality. As a result, Mrs Holland of 71 Elgar Road received a very special double Christmas present. Her husband Alfred had been recalled at the start of the war and been sent straight to the front. She received a telegram from the War Office informing her of her husband's death in action on 17 September followed by a letter of sympathy from Lord Kitchener. Her husband had taken out a life insurance policy in April with the London and Manchester Industrial Assurance Company. Upon receipt of the documents, they immediately paid his widow the sum she was entitled to – £25. A later telegram confirmed that he had been wounded and taken prisoner and was recovering in a camp in Germany. The company did not ask for a refund.

Another story, similar but different, a soldier, officially dead but in fact alive. Sergeant C. Bennett, serving with the Norfolks, was at home in Reading recovering from wounds. He received no pay because he

The war did not stop the introduction of a new bus route. This was the first run of the Kentwood Hill route in Tilehurst.

was officially dead, however, he had been wounded twice and hospitalised in Aldershot. To prove he was alive he had to go to the Regimental depot in Norwich, to be identified by an officer and then needed an employer, clergyman and a police officer to submit that he was alive. In his previous service, in China, he had also been recorded dead, after contracting enteric fever, but was later picked up alive and recovered.

Many people received news that was far from joyous. In late October, Private H. Grubb of 33 Brook Street had gone missing. Just before Christmas, they received a letter from his workmate and friend, Private J. Colyer, a GWR employee, describing the death of a son they still thought was missing. 'I am sorry to tell you the poor fellow was shot out here in Belgium at a place near Ypres, called Zonnebeke, on October 26th. He belonged to my company. Some of our mates tried to get to him, and get the watch, etc., that he had on him, but although he was not far away there was no chance of getting near him. It was death to anyone who tried to get him. I was very sorry when he was shot, because we were mates, but I have had so many mates wounded or killed.' Official notification was received only after the Christmas holiday.

As always at Christmas, alcohol played its part in the local news. William Purdue, of 109 Grange Avenue, a soldier in 4 Battalion, was granted custody of his son and a separation from his wife because she was a habitual drunkard. One drunk, Richard Palk of 79 Beecham Road, was lucky to have survived to see Christmas. He was rescued from the Kennet by 16-year-old George Ward whose valour was reported to the Royal Humane Society. Henry Liddiard serving in 10 KOYLI, was sentenced to a month in Reading Gaol; his offence was that he forced himself on and kissed a girl leaving the bathroom at the Gordon Temperance Hotel where he was billeted.

Reading's grim poverty levels have already been mentioned. Further proof of the financial state of many in the town was shown by a report concerning the 1906 Provision of Meals Act which was designed to safeguard the health of future generations. In the borough, 1114 children were receiving free meals at the Education Committee Centres where three meals a day were prepared six days a week: 1092 dinners, 476 breakfasts and 257 teas. However, this was a drop on the October figure of 1305 children. The meals were prepared in the kitchens at Tudor Road, Southampton Street and in Tilehurst, but served in eight other centres: Carey Street Baptist schoolroom, Tudor Street Soup

Christmas at Battle Hospital, then known officially as No. 1 War Hospital, Reading.

Santa Claus, distributing gifts in the infants department of Caversham Council School in Harley Road. The buildings are now Thamesmead School.

Kitchen, the Old British Schoolroom (Southampton Street), Cumberland Road Primitive Methodist Schoolroom, Elm Park Hall, The West Institute in Caversham and in Tilehurst National School.

What did they get to eat? A typical winter meal would consist of soup, followed by a pudding, while in the summer it could be bread and cheese or hashed meat, gravy and potatoes with a pudding after.

Children were aware of the changes that were occurring and felt a responsibility to help. George Palmer School recorded that they closed for Christmas on 18 December and at 3 pm ordinary work was suspended to allow the children to have games and enjoy 'gifts of sweets from a miniature Father Christmas'. They also decided to forfeit 'their toys in favour of the Belgian children' so there was money to send them cake and Christmas Puddings instead.

The troops stationed in and around the town fared very well over Christmas. A Christmas meal was provided at the Corn Exchange and Vincent's Garage for men of 7 and 8 battalions, and there was evening entertainment by the YMCA. However, this was not the case for every Berkshire unit. In one Reading family, the father was serving in the National Reserve on the Isle of Wight, and the son was with 5 Royal

Berks at Shorncliffe. There was little similarity in their two Christmas meals. Guarding prisoners on a ship near Ryde, the father had a 'very miserable Christmas Day, up at 6 a.m., breakfast porridge, small bread roll & butter. Dinner, one potato with coat on and two ounces of meat, half a cup of soup and a small piece of bread. Paid 4d for a glass of ale. Tea was a roll and butter, 1 oz of jam, ½ pint of tea and no supper.' His son, in training, was given for 'breakfast, ham and pickles, dinner, roast turkey, roast beef, potatoes, parsnips, bread, plum pudding, mince pies, two pints of beer for every man, cigarettes, apples, oranges, nuts, tea, bread and butter and cake.'

Belgian families at Sutherlands, on Christchurch Road, Reading.

The 7th Royal Berkshires enjoying Christmas dinner in the Corn Exchange, Market Place, Reading.

At the front, Gunner Southern of 85 Whiteknights Road, serving in the Royal Horse Artillery, wrote home on Boxing Day to describe his Christmas: 'We had a decent Christmas considering our position. On the 24th I played football for "A" sub-section against "B" sub-section. We had an enjoyable game and were beaten 3-0. Reveille was at 7 a.m. on Christmas Day, and following some sports we paraded for the Royal Christmas card and Princess Mary's Christmas present. At 5 p.m. we had our Christmas dinner of roast pork and vegetables, Christmas pudding in tins, and ½ lb. of chocolate a piece. Then in the evening we had an enjoyable concert. I may say that on the 24th terrific artillery fire was heard all day but Christmas and Boxing Day were quiet.'

Christmas cheer for children entitled to free meals was provided by the Education Committee on Christmas and Boxing Day. The Central Boys' School at Katesgrove was requisitioned as a packing depot and the teachers in the elementary schools were asked to volunteer as packers of the gift-bags; thirty were requested and eighty came forward. On Christmas morning the bags were delivered to eight feeding centres in Reading, Tilehurst and Lower Whitley. Two types of bag had been packed: there were 623 for those entitled to one meal a day and 521 of the bigger bag for those having two or three meals a day. While the 6d bag contained two sausages, a slice of cake, and a packet of biscuits, the 1/- had the same and also a ½ lb. of cake, two packets of biscuits and 2d bar of chocolate.

No Christmas is complete without a cracker joke. This one is from 1914. 'Why is Kulture spelled with a K in Germany? Because Great Britain has command of the Cs.'

Employees of Suttons serving with the colours received some Christmas cheer. By December, seventy-five employees were either at the front or in training. Suttons, a benevolent employer, sent each a gift of £1.

With Christmas over, the army focussed its efforts locally on improving recruiting figures with a march through Reading, with a band playing and detachments from the 4 (Reserve) and 8 battalions marching behind, hoping to attract volunteers for both units. Starting at 2.30 pm on 29 December, the detachments marched from the station, along Station Road, Queen Street, Broad Street, Oxford Road, Kensington Road, Tilehurst Road, Castle Street, Bridge Street, Southampton Street, Mount Pleasant, Silver Street, London Road,

Queen's Road, King's Road, Broad Street, West Street, and finally Friar Street to the Corn Exchange. This does not appear to have been a success – a lot of effort for no return, in fact.

It rained or snowed on twenty-three days during December 1914. The worst weather came on Monday 24th, when it rained heavily from midday into the evening. The wind then blew with hurricane force, and for two hours a violent snowstorm raged, ending very suddenly. The wind caused great damage. On the London Road near Shepherds Hill House, an uprooted tree delayed traffic. A chimney stack was blown through the roof of a business house in town, happily without causing injury. The snow melted and the Kennet, Loddon and Thames rivers flooded thousands of acres and Caversham Meadows and the biscuit factory recreation ground disappeared. Roads were submerged; some, like Church Lane in Shinfield, and parts of Arborfield Road and Three Mile Cross became impassable.

The bad weather on Boxing Day postponed the whippet racing but did not affect foxhunting – the South Berkshire Foxhounds, The Garth Hounds and The Vine Hounds were able to run three or four meetings in the week.

DORA regulations came into play in an episode in the closing days of the year. Alfred Seymour was charged with loitering for two hours in the subway at Reading station. He refused to move on, claiming that he was waiting for the train to Newbury even though the last one had left. He used very foul language when asked to move. On arrest he said he had no bad purpose but was merely waiting for the train. The chairman of the magistrates was lenient to him. Instead of £100 or six months in prison, he fined him no more than 10s and costs, with fourteen days in default.

The *Chronicle* summed up the year in its leader of 28 December: 'The year 1914 will stand in our annals as a year of ordeal. As such it passes into history unwept but not unhonoured.' But more men were still needed to secure victory. The great resolution for the New Year was 'I will be a man and enlist to-day.'

CHAPTER 2

1915
Deepening Conflict

The feature writer of the *Chronicle* summed up the past and future: 'We stand at the beginning of the New Year. The year that has passed brought us grief and loss, robbed many and many a home of the Christmas light and life, left fatherless many a child, added the weight of inconsolable sorrow to many a father's weight of years, struck at many a mother's heart with the most cruel weapon that bereavement can use, and left many a widow to cling to faith in the agony of despair…we could not rejoice in the Christmastide of 1914. But we can and do hope, and that with a great confidence. The darkest hours are passed, and there is a glow that we can all discern in the dawn of

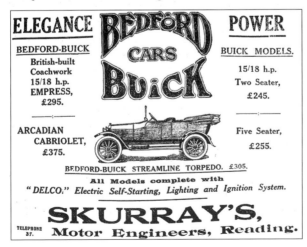

Luxurious cars and no shortage of petrol in 1915. For those who could afford it motoring was still a part of life.

New Year party given to the men of the 7th and 8th battalions by Broad Street Congregational Church. The church is now a bookstore.

the New Year. We have been chastened but we have not been found wanting.' With this in mind, the papers carried adverts for the January sales.

As the first men marched off, everyone thought it would be 'over by Christmas'. But the first Christmas of the war had come and gone, and there was no let-up in the casualties. Each week the paper carried a casualty list of those dead, killed, died of wounds, wounded, missing or prisoners of war.

The families of those missing endured a lengthy period before the War Office accepted that the soldier was dead. During that time, families tried desperately to find out any news they could and requests like these appeared in the papers: 'Information wanted. Mr and Mrs G. W. Andrews, of 70, Albert Street, Slough, would be grateful for any news of their son, L/Cpl G. P. 1975 of A Squadron, Berkshire Yeomanry, reported missing in Gallipoli on August 21st.' And again, 'Mrs Beesley of Canal Cottage, Langley New Town, will be grateful for any info as to Cpl. Beesley 16592, 5th Battalion OXBLI, reported missing.'

Families of those taken prisoner could at least look forward to being re-united at some time in the future. For some it would be over four years. Mr and Mrs Edmunds of Ivy Lodge in Twyford knew their son,

Sunday inspection of Reading's Special Constables by the mayor of Reading.

Captain C.T. Edmunds, RAMC, who had been captured at the start of the war, was a prisoner in Magdeburg Camp. On 12 January, they received a pleasant surprise when their son arrived home. He was one of five British Army doctors who had been released on 10 January. The question of who should have been released had been 'settled by drawing of lots by matches'.

Receipt of the official telegram informing them their relative was a PoW, followed by a letter from them, allowed families to get on with their lives in reasonable confidence that they would see their son, husband, father again. PoW camp censorship was strict so the sender could only write a few bland words. A typical letter was sent by Private Walker of the Coldstream Guards to his mother who lived at 70 Catherine Street. He was in Schneidemuhl Camp. 'I am in the best of health and spirits under the circumstances. We are being fairly well treated by the Germans, though, of course, we feel it very much being parted from home and wives, and children. With longing wishes for peace.' He had done his bit for the second time, having served in the South African War.

Reading's first loss occurred on 1 January. In a thirty-foot swell, HMS *Formidable*, hit by two torpedoes, rolled over on many of the crew and sank just before 5 am. Amongst the dead was 21-year-old Royal Marine Lance Corporal Ernest Nobes of 128 Elgar Road. The parents of Frederick Clift of 123 Wolseley Street received better news. He was one of the 233 survivors.

Another early death was Private Chapman of 44 Coley Terrace, a reservist who had been called up and sent straight to the front where he was wounded by shrapnel. After recovering in a Cambridge hospital, he returned home where his 'health gradually gave way and he died on 5th January' (on 7 January according to the CWGC). He was given a military funeral, something that was becoming a more and more common event.

Four missing men who worked together at the gas works and joined the Rifle Corps together. Research shows that only one of them was killed in action on 30 July, the day they disappeared, Rifleman Whye on the right.

Even in death though, everyone was not equal. Six weeks later, a funeral of more significance took place in Earley. Brigadier General M.B.F. Kelly, CB, DSO, MID, Officer in Charge of the Royal Artillery Southern Coast Defences at Portsmouth, was buried with the 'Last Post' at the end of a simple ceremony. His coffin had been met at Earley Station by 100 soldiers of the DLI and a bugle band from Portsmouth.

The most notable death of the year occurred in May, when Lieutenant R.W. Palmer, heir to the Palmer fortune, was killed in France, shot by a sniper. His position in Reading society is shown by the large number of column inches written over the weeks afterwards. 'He was a young man with an assured position, as the heir to the Right Honourable G. W. Palmer, and of high character and great personal charm. How sincerely his loss is deplored by his battalion is indicated by the letters which have come to hand. At the Reading Biscuit Factory he was looked up to and admired. His reputation in the field of sport was world-wide.' He had been capped for rugby on seventeen occasions. This extract is only a brief indication of what appeared in the papers at the time.

Lieutenant Poulton-Palmer, aged twenty-five, was killed in action on 4 May 1915.

In contrast there were no comments on the individual qualities of the two soldiers from more ordinary families in the brief report on their death. Private J. Sherwood, 42 Granby Gardens, was hit below the heart by a bullet and died within half an hour, and Private J.A. Earley who was killed almost exactly to the hour, five weeks after landing in France. He was hit by a ricochet.

A staged photo to show how the wounded arrived and were dealt with at the Royal Berkshire Hospital. The stretcher bearers are non-military volunteers.

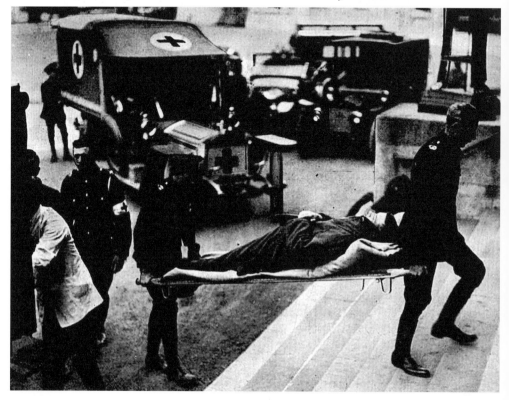

Berkshire VAD ambulances outside their headquarters on the corner of Friar Street.

Suicide and work-place deaths appeared regularly in the papers. In the same edition as the above, three deaths, two suicides and a fatal fall, were reported. Housekeeper Mrs Annie Leighford took her life by taking carbolic poison before she cut her throat and attempted to strangle herself. Eighteen-year-old Alfred Elliott of 48 Brighton Road cut his throat in the toilet – there was no obvious reason. With no Health and Safety Executive, work accidents were more common than now. Experienced painter and decorator Charles Austin of Waldeck Street fell from a plank whilst at work. The cause of death was laceration of the brain following the skull fracture and a resulting complication, pneumonia.

Whether the following report is completely true is impossible to know, though it was reported in the *Chronicle*. The Canadians had a more lenient view on such matters and it happened before repatriation was forbidden, so perhaps it is. It is certainly a fact that CSM Smith was buried in Reading Cemetery after a very unusual funeral. CSM H.G.L. Smith of the Canadian Army was buried with a three volley salute by a firing party from his regiment, followed by the 'Last Post'. What made this unusual was that he had died in No. 2 Stationary Hospital, Boulogne. Somehow his sister had managed to get his body back, contrary to the regulations stating that no one who died on active service outside the country would be repatriated by the state.

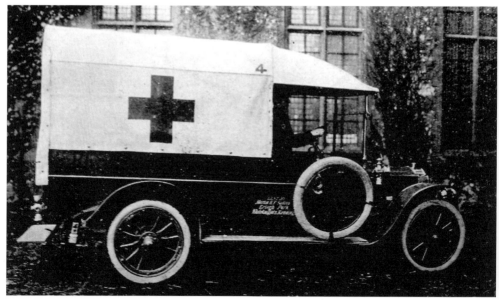

Ambulance donated by Martin Sutton of Erleigh Park, Whiteknights, Reading.

It is a given that death accompanies war; a soldier hopes that if he is to die it is in battle. For many in the Great War this was not the case. As in 1914, disease and accidents claimed their share, and many died without reaching the front. George William East, a 26-year-old Londoner, serving with 8 Royal Berks, was buried in Reading Cemetery on 3 March. Vernon Field, of 602 Oxford Road, serving in the RAMC at Wareham, when he contracted meningitis, died at the Cornelia Hospital in Poole. He was buried with full military honours at St George's Cemetery in Tilehurst.

Inevitably some families suffered more than others. The sufferings of a family from Cholsey, fifteen miles north of Reading, is typical of the experiences of many others. Possibly the first casualty was Private 1985 Alfred Abdey, of 4 Battalion who died, aged twenty, of a malignant disease of the lung on the day he should have entrained for Reading with his fellow Territorials. His brother-in-law John Alder, whose wife Lucy was pregnant, landed in France on 12 September and was killed by a shell on 5 January. Two months later, his son was born and named Alfred John Festubert Alder, after her brother and husband and the place of his death. Later in the year, she was to lose her brother Herbert during the Battle of Loos.

Often the wound or death notice gave details of the man's service, how he was wounded or killed, age, pre-war employment, family position, address, and often a note from an officer that knew him. Private Cottrell of the 1st Battalion was wounded in the right arm but went on to bayonet two Germans and shoot one. Sometimes the amount of information would be too much for the modern reader. Corporal James Darling, son of Mr and Mrs Darling of 25, Mundesley Street, serving with 2 RS, died in hospital in Belgium from wounds received near Ypres. He was severely wounded in the back and chest, the wound in the back being eight inches deep.

For some families, the grief was lessened by the comfort of having one or more sons still alive. But some lost their only son. Private Reginald Cosson, a strapping 26-year-old, over six foot tall, died on 25 January. He was the only son of Mr and Mrs W.J. Cosson, of 28 Brisbane Road. Private Cosson had been mortally wounded during a fierce bayonet charge at La Bassée. He had volunteered at the start of the war and had been at the front since 4 January, serving with 2 Sussex Regiment.

1st Batt. Royal Berks Regt.

†Major A. Scott Turner.
‡Capt. H. H. Shott.
*Lieut. T. V. B. Dennis.
*Lieut. N. S. Hopkins.

Adams, Sergt. H., 81, Waverley-road.
Allen, Pte. William, 77, Mount-street.
Barlow, Pte. T., Reserve, 25, King's-road, Caversham.
Bowles, Pte. O., Bracknell.
Burrett, Pte. John Alfred, 22, Foxhill-road.
Carter, Pte. Fredk. John, 6, Alpha-street.
Chamberlain, Pte. Charles, 164, Southampton-street.
*Chambers, Pte. J., Hillcote, Pangbourne.
Cottrell, Pte. F. E., 13, Chatham-street.
Fisher, Pte. Charles John, Radstock Farm, Lower Earley.
Fisher, Pte. William, Radstock Farm, Lower Earley.
Fowler, Pte. J.
Geo, Pte. E. T., Manor Cottages, Brimpton.
Gleed, Pte. W., 32, Queen's-road, Guildford.
Goddard, Pte. Wm., 5, Long Barn-cottages.
Goodenough, Lo.-Corpl. W., 115, Goshbrook-road.
Green, Pte. John F. R., Reading.
Green, Pte. Edmund C., Reading.
Hiscock, Pte. Albert, 34, Whitley-street.
Hollingworth, Pte. H., Bracknell.
Lee, Pte. George, 3, Essex-street.
Matthews, Pte. H., Bracknell.
Millard, Pte. F.
Millard, Pte. W.
Mitchell, Pte. Henry George, 59, Collis-street.
Pottinger, Signaller F., 8, Eldon-street.
Sawyer, Lo.-Corpl. A., Beech Cottage, Aldworth.
Simpson, Alfred, 15, Spring-terrace.
Wells, Sergt. Fredk., 1, Providence-place, Oxford-road. Fought in Boer War and possesses both the Queen's and Long Service Medals.
Wooldridge, W. T., The Village, Bradfield.

In September, the first casualty list of Reading and district men appeared.

One local firm provided an essential service for those in mourning. Hedgecocks, The House for Mourning, made 'a speciality of black costumes. Dresses, skirts, blouses, etc., in every size ready for immediate wear.' It also promised customers that mourning orders took precedence over their other business and that on receipt of an order a competent fitter would be sent at once.

In the first editions of the New Year, readers were entertained by news of the truce on the Western Front. Private Brooks wrote: 'there was not much sleep on the Eve, the night being spent by the boys in the trenches cheering and singing. Some had mouth organs, the

With such severe flooding residents of Great Knolly's Street were forced to live upstairs.

Germans had a concertina and a cornet, and with a bagpipe also blown vigorously, there was plenty of cheerful noise.' Major Buchanan-Dunlop of Whitley Rise, serving with 1 Leicesters, was involved in the truce, as was Rifleman F. Maskell of 3rd Rifle Brigade. Maskell wrote to Mr T. Parsons of 3, Chester Street about his Christmas: 'I thoroughly enjoyed myself in the trenches on Christmas Day. We held a mutual truce with the Germans in front and exchanged the compliments of the season and some Xmas gifts. Some of our fellows played "footer" between the lines. Two hares got up in the morning, and it was

No fear of excessive speed during the floods in Great Knolly's Street.

laughable to see the Germans and ourselves helter-skelter after the Christmas dinner, which escaped, as shooting was barred for the day.'

The bad weather continued into the New Year. The first week of January saw the worst floods since the great flood of 1894. Parts of the town flooded: Great Knollys, Cow Lane and Vastern Road. Water engulfed houses, forcing people upstairs, taking their livestock with them. In some parts, the floods extended a mile from the rivers Kennet and Loddon. Farmhouses were cut off, and crops affected; agriculture was badly hit.

At the front, the weather was just as bad. Lance-Corporal Lowrie serving in the Machine-gun Section of 1 Royal Berks, wrote home to his mother: 'We are now doing two days in the trenches and two days out, so it will not be so hard for us now as it used to be. The trenches are in a terrible state owing to the rain. Some of our troops are fighting in water over their knees.'

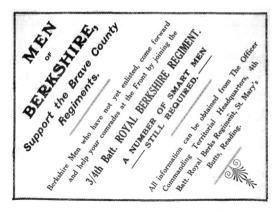

After the initial enthusiasm had waned, newer units found it more and more difficult to attract recruits from the dwindling number of available men.

The war was affecting every aspect of life but people were trying to make the best of it, as the paper noted in its short article on fox-hunting. The South Berks Hunt had been seriously hit by the war, but had endeavoured to keep going. In spite of difficulties, it had some excellent sport. They hoped the war would be over in the next year, but if it wasn't, they would make every effort to keep hunting alive in South Berks.

Another aspect affected was Empire Day, 24 May, a day when children celebrated the British Empire. The *Chronicle* reported that 'owing to the war, there will be none of the elaborate arrangements or pageants which are usually held in several of the Reading schools in celebration of Empire Day. Many head masters think that this is no season for jollity, and that the celebration should be of a religious nature, and so in several schools hymns will be sung before and after saluting the colours.'

Private Henry Liddiard, sentenced to a month for kissing a waitress at his billet, was released from Reading Gaol after serving his sentence. 'On leaving, he received his discharge from the army, a railway ticket to Pontefract where he had enlisted and a sum of money subscribed by

The children of Greyfriar's Elementary School celebrating Empire Day on 24 May.

Mrs Jarley's Waxworks performed by Wilson Senior School at the annual Children's concerts.

Organisers and Flag sellers during Wounded Soldiers' Day.

the public. A petition on the man's behalf was drawn up and received 2021 signatures in three days but the defendant was released before the effect was consummated.' He returned to his old job.

During the year the prison was emptied of prisoners who were sent to other gaols. The freed space was to be used for the internment of alien prisoners and, in later years, dissidents. 'Whilst the majority were of German origin, men of sixteen different nationalities' passed through during the course of the war. They were not prisoners so the prison regime was not as strict as for felons. Some chose to work and received payment which could be spent on un-rationed goods. They were well fed, even when food was scarce.

It seems surprising that, with so many young men in a confined area there was little sexually related crime. But what there was shows how different the legal system was a hundred years ago. Private Liddiard had been given a month for forcing himself on a woman. Twenty-six-year-old soldier, Jesse Stones, pleaded not guilty to a charge of an attempt on a minor, Lauren Beasley, who was not quite fifteen. He told the judge he was drunk at the time and was immediately acquitted, with a warning against further drunkenness or disgrace.

It was a different matter when the crime concerned two men. Two cases came up at almost the same time. Vialo Salvatore, a 37-year-old Italian organ grinder, was charged with committing an abominable offence with 16-year-old Ernest Beckett. The prisoner said he was drunk at the time and could remember nothing. He was found guilty of committing an act of gross indecency, given two months' hard labour and advised to give up drink. Benjamin Cully, a 45-year-old labourer, was indicted for attempting an unnameable offence at Reading. He pleaded not guilty but was sentenced to twelve months' hard labour.

Child abuse and sex featured in the case of Edith Appleby, of no fixed abode, a soldier's wife who was accused of shocking conduct. She was charged with neglecting Gladys Lowe (fifteen years old), Leslie Appleby (five years old) and Sidney Appleby (three years old), in a manner likely to cause them unnecessary suffering and injury to health. She pleaded guilty. Gladys had been in her care since her mother died three years ago. The other children were her own. She was receiving a separation allowance of 21s as her husband was serving with the Ox & Bucks LI in France. She admitted to leading an immoral life, consorting with soldiers and grossly neglecting her children. After selling her house, Appleby sent Lowe to live in Coley, and took her children to Pangbourne where they slept under a haystack. On return from Pangbourne, she, Lowe, Mrs Walters and a soldier slept in an empty house in Reading, which they entered through a window. Appleby had been treated for sores and her children examined by Dr Coleman. He said they were 'fairly well nourished, but filthy, and suffering from a contagious skin complaint, brought about by neglect and caused considerable suffering.' Offering no excuse, she was sentenced to three months' imprisonment with hard labour. What happened to her children? The report does not say.

Between 4 August and 31 December, 3,700 men from Berkshire had enlisted and were in training. Some 3,655 had volunteered and were waiting to be called. Even with over 7,000 volunteers, recruitment remained a major issue. The leader writer of the *Chronicle* had the answer: '1915 should be a year of general service. Service at arms by those who can give it, service in other ways at home by those who cannot take their place in what will, for all time, be remembered as the greatest voluntary army ever known…In Reading and district, there is every need for a revival of recruiting.'

Despite thousands of recruitment meetings and posters, recruiting was falling short of the needs of the services, with 1.5 million men in reserved occupations and two million men who were eligible for service but who had not volunteered. While the government opposed conscription, attestation was introduced. Men between eighteen and forty-one were canvassed and asked to attest that they would serve should they be needed. When one million single men refused to attest,

Over 200 men and NCOs of 7th and 8th battalions being entertained in the Reading YMCA prior to leaving for advanced training elsewhere.

the scheme was deemed a failure. However, in Reading, 3,546 men had responded of whom nearly half had volunteered to join the colours.

Strangely, when the mayor was asked to raise a divisional signal company for the RE with Reading in its title, there was no shortage of volunteers. Recruits were billeted at Wantage Hall until the unit was taken over by the War Office. All motorcyclist positions were filled immediately. It may well have been the pay that filled the ranks. Sappers earned from 11s 8d to 22s 2d, while pioneers and drivers received between 8s 2d and 11s 8d a week. An infantryman received 1s a day. The scheme was so successful that Reading quickly provided two companies – 32 and 35 RE Signal companies. In late October the Army Council authorised the mayor to raise a further company – 237 (Field) Coy RE (Reading).

Reg Paul (see introduction) of 237 Company RE ready for France.

In Newbury, to improve recruiting, it was decided to employ the services of Phyllis Dare, a famous musical actress. 'Kissing recruits is the latest way of getting men to serve their country…each of the forty-seven who volunteered received a kiss and every fifth man a watch…Miss Dare kissed two of the recruits.'

It was a national problem that a national newspaper tried to help

Royal Engineers in training completing a bridge across the Thames between Wargrave and Shiplake Meadows.

Trooper Quartermaine from Reading working with horses in Cairo.

solve. The '*Weekly Dispatch*' was giving a memorial cross, designed by Sir George Frampton, R.A., to the town or village which sent the largest percentage of its population to fight. The *Chronicle* gave statistics for some of the smaller Berkshire villages and left the reader to do the maths.

	Population	Enlisted
Ardington	472	47
Blewbury	564	70
Chaddleworth	347	50
Clifton Hampden	303	37
East Hanney	378	58
East Hendred	726	115
Ipsden	234	31
Little Wittenham	113	12
Lyford	112	15
North Stoke	169	20
Remenham	498	52
Sparsholt	335	59
Steventon	811	88
West Hanney	423	36

When you have a shortage, the easiest way to reduce it is to lower standards, which is what happened. There was a lack of volunteers for the Royal Navy and Royal Marines so to get recruits the requirements were lowered. The advert read, in capitals: 'Standard for boys lowered again – Age 15¾ to 18, height 5′ 1″, chest 31½. Boys who are as much as 2″ under height and 1½″ under chest can be entered if otherwise suitable.'

Marching through Reading headed by the newly formed band. The 8th Battalion is joined by youthful recruits some of whom may well be conscripted.

Corporal T.V. Gerrard married Miss Gertrude E. Rose on 9 March at St. Mary's Church. He was one of the first airmen to fly to France on the outbreak of the war.

Your King and Country Need You.

Will you answer your Country's Call? Each day is fraught with the gravest possibilities, and at this very moment the Empire is on the brink of the greatest war in the history of the world.

In this crisis your Country calls on all her young unmarried men to rally round the Flag and enlist in the ranks of her Army.

If every patriotic young man answers her call, England and her Empire will emerge stronger and more united than ever.

If you are unmarried and between 18 and 30 years old will you answer your Country's Call? and go to the nearest Recruiter— whose address you can get at any Post Office, and

Join the Army To=day !

Posters in the street and adverts in the papers asked single men to join the army.

Two local units competing for recruits from the ever-decreasing number of potential volunteers were the 3rd/1st Berkshire Yeomanry and the 3rd/4th Royal Berks. They wanted men aged nineteen to thirty-eight who were over five foot three. The incentive to join these units was that, as Territorials, they would not have to wait for their uniform.

Reading Citizens' Recruiting Committee decided to enlist the support of the women of Reading by appealing to them with a large advert on the front page of the 14 May edition of the *Chronicle*. This was The DON'T Campaign: 'DON'T FAIL TO URGE MEN OF MILITARY AGE, especially single men, to enlist at once – THE COUNTRY NEEDS THEIR SERVICES NOW. DON'T HESITATE

TO SEND THE NAMES AND ADDRESSES of those who should join to the Recruiting Officer, at Station Road, Reading. Your letter will be treated confidentially. DON'T PUT OBSTACLES IN THE WAY of those who are anxious to enlist – encourage them to serve their King and Country. DON'T INSIST UPON THE SAME EFFICIENT SERVICE as you have been accustomed to receive from your tradesman – this obviously is impossible, as a large percentage of their best men are engaged upon active service. DON'T ASK YOUR TRADESMEN TO MAKE UNNECESSARY JOURNEYS TO YOUR HOUSE – a postcard overnight, a telephone message before the first delivery, and allowing your servant to fetch goods for immediate requirements, will help them considerably, and should not inconvenience you. DON'T FORGET THAT READING STILL HAS A GREAT NUMBER OF ELIGIBLE SINGLE MEN WHO HAVE NOT ANSWERED THEIR COUNTRY'S CALL. PREVAIL UPON THEM TO DO SO IMMEDIATELY.'

An advert carried by papers across the country. 'Real men volunteer'.

Recruits were supposed to be a minimum of eighteen on enlistment. This rule was widely disregarded and many boys joined the colours, some with their parents' permission. Often the real age only came out when one was killed. The 16 July edition of the *Chronicle* carried a brief note about Rifleman W. Diaper of Mill Lane, Easthampstead. His platoon sergeant had notified his sister of his death. He had joined on 22 March and was one of thirteen volunteers for a draft sailing on 1 June. He was seventeen years old on 15 April; he met his death on 6 July.

Although many men still were not in the army, shops and factories were finding it difficult to get staff. The manpower shortage led to a change in work and life patterns. One Reading store came up with an idea to help improve its service even with the shortages. 'Gregory, Love, & Co. Ltd., begged to announce that, due to a very depleted staff through enlistment, they were obliged to consider a method of offering their best service while economising in working hours.' Normally the dinner break was distributed between 11.30 and 2.30 but from Monday,

Members of 177 and 178 Company of the ASC (MT) in fancy dress at the sports day held in Palmer Park during the summer of 1915.

17 May they had decided to close for a dinner hour for the whole staff between 1.15 and 2.15 daily. This meant that the maximum number of staff were available during the busiest hours. This was not an original idea, but an action which was being adopted throughout the country.

Reading's hairdressers also changed their hours. Fifty-six of them signed an application to the Sanitary Committee, urging a closing order to be made under the Shops Act. They wanted standardised closing times for all hairdressers in the borough with 8.00 pm. on Monday, 9.00 pm on Tuesday, Thursday and Friday, 11.00 pm on Saturday, 1.00 pm on Wednesday (weekly half-holiday) and all day Sunday.

Although enlistment had fallen considerably, Reading and the immediate area was awash with soldiers from other parts of the country. Reading housed the regimental depot with new recruits and staff, plus two battalions of the Royal Berks waiting for the construction of billets on Salisbury Plain. At the end of January, Wokingham was 'full of troops'. On 22 January, 10 NF arrived from Aldershot to be billeted in the town and at Emmbrook to undertake battalion training, a total number of 1,156 NCOs and men with thirty-four officers. Already there were thirty-seven officers and 1,160 NCOs and men of 13 DLI, making well over 4,000 soldiers in a very small area.

Numbers were rapidly reduced when sufficient huts had been built on Salisbury Plain. In May, the two remaining Royal Berks battalions, billeted in the town, received orders to move. The departure of 7 Battalion was reported at some length. It left Reading in three batches, at 9.10 am, 10.20 am and noon. There were crowds in the street to watch the soldiers march to the station 'with their full equipment on their backs and rifles on their shoulders, each company with an officer at the head. As they passed into the station, greetings, farewells and handshakes were exchanged with female friends, some of whom made their way to the platform, where there were some affectionate farewells. All the men had a healthy, tanned look and appeared to be in the best of health and spirits. To the accompaniment of hearty cheers the different contingents left Reading. The contingent which left at noon were a joyous crew. At the far end they were in such high spirits that, after a sweetheart was kissed, all the rest clamoured for one – and got it. So did the next three carriages.'

The coffee stall at Reading S.E. & C.R. Station for soldier and sailor passengers. It was opened in May and run by the Berkshire Womens Volunteer Corps, affiliated to the Red Cross. Funds were provided by subscription, and voluntary donations from local companies.

There were also numbers of German soldiers near Reading. Philberds House at Holyport, Maidenhead, was a prison camp housing 100 officers and 40 other ranks as servants, guarded by Devon territorials. It was the scene of a number of escapes. The first attempt was foiled in April when the Adjutant, Captain Armstrong, became suspicious of the amount of gardening taking place behind the mansion and especially the number of raised flower beds. He got an outsider to lay drains in the area, and soon a pick hit something solid, a twelve yard long, two foot square wood-supported tunnel. Using a fire shovel, the Germans had cut through the concrete foundation of the outer wall and were nearly out of the grounds.

Enemy aliens had been placed in internment camps across the country. One can only wonder why nobody thought to point out the fact that the Royal Family were Germans. The Anti-German Union was formed to fight against German influences in British social, financial, social and political life. Among its vice-presidents were members of the aristocracy. It was on the front page of the *Chronicle* at the beginning of June. Shortly afterwards, Prince Christian and his wife, Princess Victoria of Schleswig-Holstein, attended the Windsor Rose show in the grounds of the castle. The king, a patron of the society, presented a Challenge Cup for the Best 48 Distinct Single Truss. Interestingly, there was no comment from the anti-German Union about this and it would be two years before the monarch denounced his German origins and titles.

Alcohol had been seen as a problem before the war. With around 200,000 convictions per annum, it was an issue that needed to be controlled. In March 1915, Lloyd George clearly stated his position on the matter: 'We are fighting Germany, Austria and Drink, and, as far as I can see, the greatest of these deadly foes is drink.' In Reading Charles Stevens, a 44-year-old labourer had been sentenced to a month's hard labour. His crime: attempting suicide with a razor while drunk. The chairman of the magistrates told Stevens that he hoped the sentence would be a warning to him. Elizabeth Young of 51 Mount Street admitted being drunk in the Oxford Road. She was so drunk she had to be taken to the police station by ambulance. She was placed on probation for twelve months. William Elliott of 48 Brighton Road was fined 5/- for being helplessly drunk. He could remember nothing about it. The *Chronicle* classed Flossie Archer, of 6, Sackville Street, as a sad

An advert that many loyal citizens probably felt duty-bound to take note of. Support the war effort, drink more spirits.

case. She was charged with being drunk in Baker Street, pleading guilty. According to PC Blake, she was lying helplessly drunk on the footway and he had to get assistance to convey her to the station. She was remanded on her undertaking to place herself under the care of Miss Messenger, the Court Missionary, while inquiries were made as to what could be done for her. Such occurrences were relatively few and, as the war progressed, the figures fell and Reading became known as a very sober town.

Alcohol and child neglect featured in the case of Mary Butcher of 92 Great Knollys Street. She was charged on remand with neglecting four children aged three to ten. It was not the result of poverty. She received a 29s separation allowance because her husband was in the ASC and a further 2s from her son in the navy. Owning a small shop with an attached off-licence added to her income. The problem – 'she had given way to drink'. As a result she 'had so neglected her children that they got into a terrible condition.' Dr Coleman found the children with 'verminous heads, scantily clothed, and in a most filthy condition from dirt, so as to greatly threaten their health'. He ordered their removal to a Poor Law Institution. 'The case was the most appalling that had come before the bench,' said the chairman. As Mary Butcher wept copiously, she was imprisoned for four months with hard labour.

Mary Butcher's case was not unique. Elizabeth Tedder of 77 Wolseley Street pleaded guilty to neglecting her children. Although she was drawing war allowances of 33s 7d per week she had allowed the family of four children to sink into a disgraceful state of neglect while she drank to excess.

Later in the year, Lloyd George, in the House of Commons, paid glowing tribute to the 'patriotic spirit' of the licensed trade. A War Service Census taken earlier by the Reading and District Licensed Traders' Protection and Benevolent Association showed that 566 members and their sons had enlisted. Twenty had already sacrificed their lives in the defence of the realm. By October the number was around 800, with 400 more from the local breweries, including a number of directors.

Petty crime continued to cover many column inches in the papers. Some minor misdemeanours received severe punishment. A 16-year-old with a previous conviction was given six weeks' hard labour for stealing a bike lamp. George Cripps of Whitley Wood Lane, who did not bother to turn up for his trial, was fined 7s 6d or seven days for riding a bicycle without a light. Tom Smith of York Road was fined 10s and costs for using obscene language near his house and Dudley Hazell, a cadet at RMC Sandhurst, had his licence suspended for six months and was fined £10 with 10s 6d costs for riding his motorcycle at a speed dangerous to the public between Emmbrook and Wokingham on the Reading Road.

Boys will be boys regardless of whether there is a war on or not, and sometimes they do something they later regret. Seven boys appeared in court for throwing stones. Unfortunately for them, they were good shots. Harry Lewington needed stitches on his forehead as a result. Three were discharged because of a lack of evidence, the others pleaded guilty and were fined 5s each. Later in the year, four small boys were each fined 5s for stoning a kitten to death.

Not only men and boys appeared before the Bench. Lucy Youlton, a respectably dressed woman of 47 George Street, was charged and convicted of shoplifting three pairs of ladies' shoes with a value of 28s 9d. She was bailed on surety of £20 and a £10 surety from her husband. An unnamed 15-year-old girl who stole a half-sovereign appeared before the Bench. It was her first offence so she was discharged with a warning about ruining her future. Elizabeth Somner of 29 Vachel Road was placed on probation for three years. She had been 'found wandering and behaving in an indecent manner in Abbot's Walk'.

Even with so many men in the army, there was still serious crime. In late February came a mini-epidemic of burglary. Three houses were entered and property stolen. Twenty-five shillings and a gold locket were stolen from 44 Radstock Road and the front door bolted against anyone entering. The same modus operandi was used at 8 Radstock Road where the burglars opened a safe and took a gold bracelet and a boy's watch and chain, before leaving through the back door. In the time it took the owners to go to the station and return, burglars had entered 47 St Bartholomew's, ransacked two bedrooms, stolen a brooch, a lady's watch-glass, a chain and a new pair of suede gloves. The stolen purse contained no money and was later found with the contents intact in a London Road garden.

However, overall, the war seemed to have a positive effect on crime rates. The Chief Constable of the Reading Constabulary was able to write in his yearly report: 'During the past year the number of indictable and non-indictable offences shows a very satisfactory decrease compared with previous years. There is little doubt that the war has something to say for this, and that a high conception of duty has taken hold of the people in the present crisis.' Similarly, his return for the first quarter of the year showed a general reduction on comparable rates in the same quarter last year. Burglary, housebreaking and simple larceny had decreased, but there had been an increase in obtaining goods by false pretences.

There was only a single really serious case in 1914, wilful murder, and that occurred just before the war started. A mother had murdered her 6-year-old daughter, attempted to murder her 4-year-old daughter, and then committed suicide. In 1915 there was also one murder. Frederick Kirkpatrick of 32 Westfield Road, Caversham, murdered his wife and then committed suicide. Private Cole, billeted with the couple, heard shouting. Mrs Fitzpatrick ran into his room, fell on the bottom of his bed and died. After he had slashed his wife's neck as she sat, Mr Fitzpatrick went into the garden and cut his neck from ear to ear. The coroner returned a verdict of murder and suicide while temporarily insane.

Infanticide was to appear in the local papers a number of times during the war. It had appeared before in the 1890s when Amelia Dyer had made her living by killing unwanted children. 'In those days infant mortality was high and children's lives were cheap.' Finding a hastily-disposed child rated only a small space in the paper. On 12 May, a cadet at the RMC Sandhurst was boating on the lake. He spotted a box in the water and recovered it. Inside was the body of a female child. The head was tightly bound round with calico, and there were two pieces of brick and some coal ashes in the box. Post-mortem investigations suggested the child had died a week previously and had probably been suffocated. The inquest was adjourned to enable the police to pursue their inquiries but these came to nothing. Could such a crime go unpunished in the 21st century? How long would the police search for the parent(s)?

Did life really mean so little? Later in the year there was a similar case in Reading. In December, a newly-born male child was found in two bags on waste ground at the junction of Dorset Street and Gordon Place. The only clue at the scene was a quantity of spent matches. The cause of death was partial suffocation through want of attention at birth.

There were thieves in the army as well. Henry Langford of the 4th Royal Berks was charged and convicted of the theft of 5s from the house he was billeted in. Acting on a suspicion, Sergeant-Major Graham had marked the coins in the house that were later found in Langford's possession. He was classed as not a very good character from a military point of view but he had no prior convictions. Fined £1 or fourteen days, the money would be stopped out of his pay. Of this invasion of men, the Chief Constable was able to report that although there had been an increase in army and navy non-indictable offences, mostly AWOL cases, their conduct was generally very good.

Military offences were not confined to enlisted men. May saw the court-martial of two officers, 2nd Lieutenant Blackall and 2nd Lieutenant Thompson of 8 Battalion. In the court, presided over by Brigadier-General Stewart, and held in the lecture room of the Reading Gas Company in Friar Street, the two men were accused of a range of offences. Blackall was charged with absenting himself without leave from his billet and from all duties and parades for four days. Thompson was charged with disobeying a superior officer, failing to take Blackall under close arrest to his room and staying with him until relieved, and allowing him to leave his room and accompany him in the street, as well as being drunk in the officers' mess. After weeks of deliberation, the court reached a decision. Blackall was to be reprimanded.

The Royal Berks Hospital and many large private houses were already in use for wounded troops but there were plans to further expand the number of beds available. The answer, to military minds, was simple, take over schools. Early attempts to do this had been resisted, but with so many casualties there was now little choice.

The *Chronicle* told its readers that large numbers of wounded soldiers would be arriving in the town on a date still unspecified but their destination was settled. 'Elementary Schools and public buildings

Some of the first wounded to arrive at Reading for treatment at the Royal Berkshire Hospital. The vehicles are Ford motor ambulances provided by the Wellington Club.

are to be adapted as hospitals…Efforts are being made to interfere as little as possible with the education of the children attending the elementary schools concerned, but in some cases it has been necessary to institute a system of 'half-time', the morning session being from 8.30 to 12.30 and the afternoon session from 1.30 to 5. 'Half-time' meant that one school would take the children of another school for half the day. This meant running special tram cars for the children. Wilson Road went to Wokingham Road, Battle went to Swansea Road, Grovelands to Tilehurst and Redlands to Newtown. To help transport the wounded, Mr Martin Sutton of Erleigh Park in Whiteknights, lent an ambulance.

University College offered its buildings but they were turned down. They would be used later for training engineers, munitions workers and the RFC.

Initially the war hospitals reported their cases but as numbers increased the data ceased. Below are the cases in four of the hospitals.

Wounded heroes	No. 1 war hospital	No. 2 Battle Schools	No. 4 Redlands School	Royal Berks Hospital
Dangerously wounded	1	-	-	-
Severely wounded	34	-	-	11
Slightly wounded	29	17	2	8
Severely sick	2	-	4	3
Slightly sick	23	30	27	3

To provide eggs for the wounded, a national egg collection had been established. Collected eggs were deposited centrally and distributed to hospitals. At Easter, a special effort was made to collect even more than usual, so everyone could have eggs during Easter week. Locally the star was Mrs G. Ford at Lea Heath near Hurst. She had collected 912 eggs. It was hoped to make it up to 1,000 during the week. Reading children were collecting old newspapers in aid of the National Relief Fund. With the closing of the schools that had become hospitals, it was decided to cease collecting. On closure thirty and a half tons had been collected, which had raised £115 for the fund.

Something that would become a standard offering by those with adequate funds was the Memorial Bed. The first at the Royal Berks

No. 1 Reading War Hospital showing the Joblots, amateur entertainers who sang and played to the wounded.

Children from Cumberland Road visiting the wounded.

Ambulances waiting for the arrival of the wounded.

Staff pose with their patients at one of the convalescent hospitals in Reading.

Passing the time in a Reading War Hospital.

An Egg Fund lapel badge sold to raise money to purchase eggs for soldiers in hospital.

Hospital was in the Benyon Ward and was endowed by Mrs Bruce of Arborfield Court, in memory of her grandson. The plaque above the bed read: 'The Bruce Allfrey Bed, endowed by Jessie Anne Bruce, in loving memory of her grandson, Frederic Vere Bruce Allfrey, Lieutenant, IX Lancers, killed in action September 7th 1914, near Provins, France, in the Great War with Germany.'

As the town was becoming an important centre for war hospitals, it was decided to form a War Hospital Care and Comforts Committee. Its purpose was to help make the life of the wounded as pleasant as possible. To achieve this, it needed volunteers to look after visiting families, and provide books, papers and illustrated magazines. People were sought who would be prepared to take men for drives, have them over in their gardens and arrange entertainment in the wards. For this last requirement a special group was formed 'The Reading Favourites', who performed regularly throughout the war, entertaining thousands of men.

Reading's growing importance as a hospital town is shown by an unannounced visit by the king and queen. On 31 July, with just a few hours warning, they motored from Windsor to visit The War Hospital on Oxford Road. Can the modern reader visualise the Queen arriving in Reading without telling anyone, no time to scrub everything, to find your best clothes, prepare a speech, paint everything and make or mend anything that supposedly needs to be done for such a modern-day visit? When news leaked out large crowds formed 'to give a hearty welcome'.

The children of Cumberland Road Primitive Methodist Church taking flowers and eggs to Redlands Hospital.

Corpl. THOMAS BYRNE, 7th Batt. East Yorks Regt.

Corpl. JAMES H. BYRNE, Army Ordnance Corps.

Miss B. A. BYRNE, Nurse Sister in France.

Sergt.-Major J. BYRNE, Recruiting Sergeant.

Sergeant-Major Byrne, 34 Milman Road and his children.

Miss M. E. BYRNE, Nurse at the Dardanelles.

Corpl. PETER A. BYRNE, Army Ordnance Corps.

Bugler CHRISTOPHER A. BYRNE, 3/4th Batt. Royal Berks Regiment.

Corpl. LEONARD JOHN BYRNE, 12th Batt. King's Royal Rifle Corps.

The arrival of the King and Queen for their unannounced visit to No. 1 War Hospital on 31 July.

King George and Queen Mary making an inspection of the hospital, in company with Lieutenant Colonel Hanley, O.C., Captain J.L. Joyce, Registrar, and Miss Willetts, Matron.

The Royal car in the grounds of Reading War Hospital No. 1 during the July visit.

Three ways in which the public could help the wounded. Give money, donate materials for the manufacture of hospital necessaries or offer to help in their manufacture.

The visit was brief, and after about two hours of meeting, talking and shaking hands they returned to Windsor.

To fund this charity would need public support, there being no government money available. It was decided to have a Wounded Soldier's Day on 5 June. Money would be raised by selling the medallions and tabs designed and produced by the staff and students of the Fine Arts and Crafts Departments at the University College. Coinciding with the Wounded Soldier's Day in Oxford, it was a great success. Some 100,000 medallions were made for the day but at 11.00 am there was an emergency order for 20,000 more. Nearly 120,000 badges were sold, raising £1,286.

Later in the year came yet another flag day. This time for Russia. Around 150,000 flags were sold in Reading and the villages within fifteen miles. This effort raised £1,900 14s. Reading was proud that it had raised the highest amount taken on any Russian Flag Day in the country. The final total raised by Reading with extras was £2,142.

The Royal Berkshire Regiment, Pipe & Cigarette Fund was another

Yet another flag day, this time for Russia.

A young nurse pins a flag on to a soldier during Wounded Soldier's Day.

charity in need of financial support. It was pleased with its contribution so far: in its first year, it had sent to Royal Berks soldiers two tons of tobacco, 2,000 pipes and over a million cigarettes. It was supplying, twice a month, 800 packets containing two ounces of tobacco, thirty-

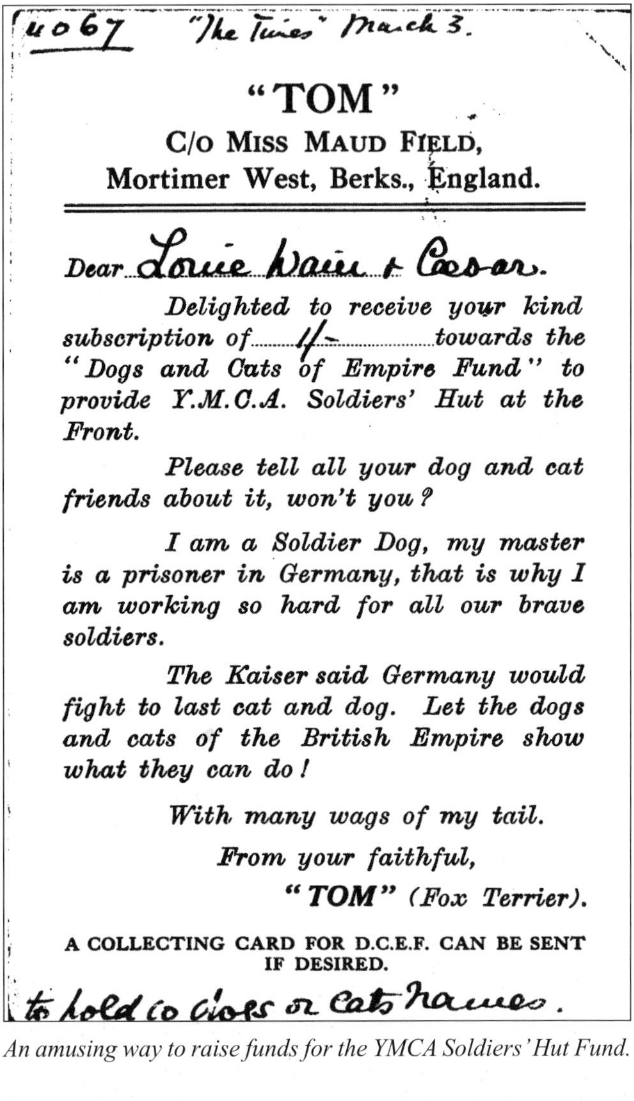

4067 *"The Times" March 3.*

"TOM"

C/O MISS MAUD FIELD,
Mortimer West, Berks., England.

Dear *Louie Wain & Cæsar.*

Delighted to receive your kind subscription of *1/–* towards the "Dogs and Cats of Empire Fund" to provide Y.M.C.A. Soldiers' Hut at the Front.

Please tell all your dog and cat friends about it, won't you?

I am a Soldier Dog, my master is a prisoner in Germany, that is why I am working so hard for all our brave soldiers.

The Kaiser said Germany would fight to last cat and dog. Let the dogs and cats of the British Empire show what they can do!

With many wags of my tail.

From your faithful,

"TOM" (Fox Terrier).

A COLLECTING CARD FOR D.C.E.F. CAN BE SENT IF DESIRED.

to hold 60 dogs or cats names.

An amusing way to raise funds for the YMCA Soldiers' Hut Fund.

five cigarettes and a supply of matches, to each of the four battalions on active service, at a cost of £160. It was also dealing with the smoking needs of the Royal Berks wounded across the country and sending 140 newspapers to each battalion weekly, viz., the *Chronicle, Reading Standard, Maidenhead Advertiser, Windsor Express* and *Newbury Weekly News*. The monthly cost was £190 but there was only

£179 to cover costs until the New Year. The sum of £1,200 was needed urgently to cover the last three months of the year. Needless to say, the money was forthcoming and the men were provided for.

Ironically, the week after the request for money from the Tobacco Fund, the *Chronicle* carried a brief comment on the death of Private John Landy of 4th NF. He had habitually smoked fifty cigarettes a day and died of heart failure. In the same issue was the news that the Reading Licensed Victuallers had responded to Sir Ian Hamilton's appeal for tobacco and cigarettes for the MEF. They had sent the town MP, Lt. Colonel Wilson, 5,000 cigars for his men. The Tobacco Fund also announced that they had just received 40,000 Manilla cigars.

Raising money locally or at a national level was a constant throughout the war. In competition with local efforts were government war loans. With their good returns, they attracted much interest, as evidenced by the report in the *Chronicle*: 'The response to the new War Loan in Reading has been excellent. On Tuesday (22 June) the Post Office and the branch offices were besieged with inquirers, and all the prospectuses and explanatory leaflets were quickly exhausted…The loan was evidently attracting all classes of society.'

As well as needing money from the citizens of Reading and men for the armed forces, the town's skilled engineering workforce was

An estimated 5,000 attended the Elm Park Carnival that raised money for the Reading Care and Comforts Committee. Here soldiers try to avoid a soaking in a game known as tilting the bucket. A total of £202 was raised.

Lieutenant General Sir Edward Bethune took the salute from the platform in front of the Town Hall on 2 October for a procession of local based troops and nurses and orderlies of the Berkshire Voluntary Aid Detachments.

The Berkshire Volunteer Regiment provided manual labour during weekends when it was not training. Here they are loading wagons at Didcot.

targeted by the government. In June a War Munitions Bureau opened at the Queen's Hotel in Friar Street. This was an attempt to get any skilled engineering worker, not already on government service, to place his services at the disposal of the country. Men registering had to sign an undertaking to signify their willingness to remove to another district at short notice and to remain in that employ for at least six months. Like the war bonds, the office did far better than expected and stayed open longer than originally intended.

As well as engineers, the Munitions Committee needed suitable space to produce munitions. Any small workshop could be approached if needed. In late August, Reading Tramways Department received a request to undertake 'certain work in the manufacture of munitions of war'. As the work would not interfere with the department's business the Town Council agreed to the request.

Books and magazines were also wanted. The papers ran requests for them to be handed in at Reading post offices for distribution to the army and navy. Since the start of the year, it was reported that the organisation had sent over 3,000 books and magazines a week but even more were needed. In case a reader wondered where their donation could have gone, its possible destination was given: 'Boxes of books and magazines are sent regularly to every unit serving with the Expeditionary Forces and to chaplains of every denomination, and to PoWs.' They were also sent to camps at home and abroad to set up libraries for the troops, and regular supplies were sent to the Reading Rooms established for women munitions workers.

Huntley & Palmers ran a war bond scheme for their employees that was copied by the GWR but not in such a generous way. They

The recruitment march through Reading in January, of 500 men of the 2nd/4th battalions, Royal Berkshire Regiment, and 8th battalions, starting in Station Road.

purchased the war bond stock and allowed their work people and clerks to acquire the bonds from them, not exceeding £25, by weekly instalments over two years. When £4 was reached, the company gave the employee £1 as a gift to complete the purchase. They would also pay interest at 5%, not the 4.5% of the government.

While the marches continued across Berkshire, in Newbury, the mayor made a personal effort to enlist more volunteers. He invited unattested men of military age to a meeting with him at Oddfellows Hall on the understanding there would be no recruiting sergeants. His aim was to recruit himself and local men to serve in the same regiment together, in imitation the 'Pals' battalions. There was little response to the mayor's request, but he did join the army and after recovering from a severe grenade wound in training, served with distinction in France where he was Mentioned in Dispatches and won the Military Cross.

With men not coming forward, it is difficult to believe that printing the following about 2 Platoon of the 1st/4th Battalion would have helped boost recruitment. 'It was a "beano" for a minute or two… lumps of tiles and bits of wood flying all over the place, as well as lots of shell.' This happened upon their return to the line after having a bath well behind the front. As it was dark, the writer and friends sat on, instead of in, their dug-out to clean their rifles. A random shell landed on the dug-out killing four Reading men outright; another Reading man died of wounds, and a further five Reading and district men were wounded, plus four others.

Not all the letters from the front were about death and destruction. One at least was a humorous portrayal of what a recruit could expect on arrival in France. It was written by Private R. Hussey, whose parents ran The Rose in Weldale Street: 'To be let. This attractive and well-built dug-out, containing one reception, kitchen, bathroom, and one up-to-date "funk-hole", (4 foot by 3 foot). All modern inconveniences, including gas and water. This desirable residence stands one foot above the water level, commanding an excellent view of the enemy's trenches; excellent shooting ("Snipe and duck"). – Particulars off the late tenant, Base Hospital.'

There were still large numbers of men able, but not prepared, to attest, and not all of those that had attested were really keen to go. The inquest on 24-year-old George Jobbins, an assistant fish fryer, clearly showed that not everyone wanted to be a soldier. He was normally very lively but after signing the National Registration paper he thought he would have to go to the war, and that preyed upon his mind. There was nothing else worrying him. He was found hanging by string to the ratchet chain on the shafts of a farm roller in Cow Lane. 'Suicide during temporary insanity' was the verdict.

Trooper N. Town of the RHG, at home on leave, was amazed, he wrote to the paper, 'to see so many young men loitering about the town, when their place should be serving with his Majesty's Forces…stronger measures ought to be taken to compel these young men to put their

When the regiments left Britain, the men kept in touch by letter. While they could not give their exact location, the photos often provided a clue. Here Berkshire Yeomanry pose in front of the Sphinx.

The National Registration in Reading showing the volume of paper involved. A staff of between forty and fifty, mostly teachers, were needed for many days to complete the task.

shoulders to the wheel.' Compulsion was only months away and with the threat of compulsory service the number of enlistments increased. The 19 November edition of the *Chronicle* gave the names of 283 who had attested but not necessarily enlisted. A week later, the paper reported 208 enlistments and the arrival of 150 men from North America who were eager to enlist. One, a native of Reading, had come from North Dakota and paid £25 to return to England to enlist in Reading to get to the front quicker.

In the same vein, a soldier on active service in Gallipoli expressed his thoughts about some of the news: 'The only thing that disheartens us is when we get papers and read about the men striking at home. You have no idea how the men here curse about them: men who have now gone to their deaths almost cursing their fellow countrymen. I always thought I was a peace-loving chap…I feel much more justified in turning a machine gun on those skulking curs than on these Turks, who after all are only doing what they consider is right…Do you know what happens to a man that strikes here? He is shot, and that is what should happen to those curs at home.'

Recruitment in Reading was still not going well. In June members of the Berkshire Regiment marched through the county in an attempt to gain recruits for the recently-formed Berkshire units. Enlistment analysis painted a poor picture of Reading's patriotism. The

Newspaper appeal for car owners to loan their cars to the army if there was an invasion. If the army had insufficient transport where would it find the drivers for these vehicles?

Berkshire Territorial Force Association.

POSSIBLE INVASION.

APPEAL TO ALL OWNERS OF MOTOR CARS.

The Berkshire Territorial Force Association has been asked by the General Officer Commanding-in-Chief, Southern Command, to approach all owners of Motor Cars in Berkshire as to whether in the possibility of an invasion they would place their cars at the disposal of the Military Authorities for the rapid transport of Troops to any spot where their services might be required.

It would be necessary for each owner to fill in the following form, which may be obtained from any Superintendent or Inspector of Police in the various districts, or the form below may be cut out and used.

BERKSHIRE TERRITORIAL FORCE ASSOCIATION.

With a view to the rapid Mobilization of Troops in case of Invasion or other serious War emergency, I, the undersigned, hereby offer to any Country the free loan of my (a)............Private Motor Car and Driver for use in the British Isles, and I further undertake to immediately carry out any instructions I may receive either per wire or otherwise.

(a) State "one" or more as the case may be.

Name of Owner ....

Address ....

Telephone No. ....

Telegraphic Address ....

Make of Car .... Rating h.p........Year.........

Registered No. .... Seats, including Driver......

Type of Body ....

Name of Driver ....

Address ....

Signed ....

Date .... 1915.

This form to be filled in and returned to the
Berkshire Automobile Club,
16, Friar Street, Reading,
who have undertaken to tabulate and register the cars.

It is obvious that at such a time the Railway Traffic would be more or less congested with the movement of troops and stores, and that the assistance suggested would be of the greatest importance, enabling a large number of troops to be moved much more rapidly than would otherwise be the case.

M. L. PORTER (Capt.), Secretary.
Berkshire County Association.
Reading.

number of recruits from the borough was running at fifty per cent of the county total. Even the territorial battalion could not raise men. After six months of recruiting it stood at just 350 men. Another issue that little could be done about was the large number of men rejected as medically unfit for service.

Not every man wanted a cushy life. While the army was struggling to get recruits, Driver H. Harris of the Berks RHA did not want to leave the army. He wrote to his aunt in Reading: 'I had the chance of coming back to England but I have signed on for another four years. I shall be given my discharge as soon as the war is ended, or, at least, as soon as they can possibly get it for me when the war is over. I feel that this is a time when every man is urgently wanted.' His battery motto was: 'we dare not think about wives or sweethearts, our mothers, dads, or sons; if we want to win our battles, we must man our blooming guns.'

G.   R.

GOD SAVE THE KING.

132nd OXFORDSHIRE HEAVY BATTERY,

ROYAL GARRISON ARTILLERY.

Recruits Wanted.

Height 5 feet 8 inches.

Pay and Separation Allowances the same as in other Batteries of the Regular Army.

JOIN AT ONCE.

Apply to Recruiting Officer, Reading.

Railway Pass supplied for purpose of Enlistment at Exeter College or Cowley Barracks, Oxford.

Every unit needed more recruits and was prepared to poach from neighbouring counties that did not have the same formations. Berkshire provided horse artillery but did not have a heavy battery.

The recent low recruitment did not dim civic pride in what had been achieved by ex-pupils of the borough schools. At a meeting of the Reading Education Committee, the clerk reported the figures relating to old boys now serving. From the council schools, 1,394 were in the army and 247 in the navy; twenty had been commissioned in the army and two in the navy; 124 had been wounded serving on land and one at sea. Sixty-three had been killed serving in the army and fourteen in the navy. One soldier had won the DCM and five had been Mentioned in Dispatches against one sailor. In the borough voluntary schools, 730 had joined the army, of whom seven had been commissioned, one promoted for bravery and one Mentioned in Dispatches; 114 joined the navy. Fifty-five soldiers had been wounded and twenty-two killed. In the navy 4 had been wounded and one killed.

At the annual Reading Boys' School speech day, the Head informed the audience that schools such as his were playing a most important part in the war and that, for its size, few schools had achieved more.

To back this up he gave some statistics: 'There were or had been 151 officers, 96 rank & file and 3 cadets in Sandhurst; total 250. 15 had forfeited their lives for their country, 3 were missing, 1 was interned in Holland, and 14 were wounded. A number had been awarded honours: Lt. Colonel J.A.S. Tulloch, the Legion of Honour, CG and MID; Captain C. St. Q. O. Fullbrook-Leggat, DSO, MC and MID (three times); the late Captain G. Belcher, the MC; Captain S. V. Shea, MID and Sergeant T.P. Norris, MID. The pupils at the time were also doing well with 16 out of 17 passing the Oxford and Cambridge entrance exams, two with scholarships. The head told the gathering that "the moral value of the war will considerably over-balance the material loss".'

Because of their patriotism and not wanting to be left out, every organisation, school or business wanted everyone to know how they had or were helping the war effort. Why the Education Department would want to know how many ex-pupils were in the forces is unclear, but in July 1915 they called for this information. The head of the Boys' Department at Redlands informed them that 'as far as he could ascertain, 79 ex-scholars of Redlands had joined the Army to date and 21 the Navy. Of these four were commissioned, 11 had been wounded and five killed.'

Another display of civic pride began at the end of August. It was

TWO READING D.C.M.'S.

(1). ACTING CO. SERGT.-MAJOR H. PIKE, 2nd K.O.S.B., of 70, Albany Road, Reading, who has received the D.C.M. for consistent gallantry in action. (2). ACTING-SERGT. E. BURGESS, of the 1st Royal Berks Regt., of Lower Armour Road, Tilehurst, who has received the D.C.M. for his part in the gallant action at Givenchy.   On February 20 he was wounded in the face, but has made excellent progress at a private house at Leicester.

Two local heroes.

'arranged to supply to the occupier of any house in Reading from where a man has enlisted in the Navy or Army a badge bearing the words: "A Man from this house is serving his King and Country".' They were intended to be displayed in the front room window, with one badge for each male serving. These badges were much prized and appeared in many windows across the borough, some houses having as many as five on display.

Reading overflowed with civic pride in December when its first VC winner was home on leave. Trooper Frederick Potts, of Edgehill Street, won his medal for bravery in Gallipoli. In recognition of his achievement, on 6 December, he 'received emphatic assurances of the admiration of his fellow townsmen' at a big civic presentation attended by the mayor and all the councillors when he received a two page vellum address in a casket.

To commemorate the first anniversary of the war, there was a united open-air service on the lawn of St John's in Victoria Square. The

Trooper Frederick William Owen Potts, the first Berkshire Yeoman to receive the Victoria Cross. This was awarded for saving a severely wounded comrade under Turkish fire while serving on Gallipoli. The photo shows Trooper Potts, his parents, sisters and brother-in-law, outside the family home at 54 Edgehill Street.

The Reading Central School became War Hospital No. 5 during 1915.

afternoon weather was fine and a 'very large assemblage of men and women of all denominations…joined reverently and heartily in a very impressive service.' Hymns included 'God the All-terrible' and 'O God, our help in ages past'. This was followed by speeches, the Benediction and the singing of the National Anthem. In the evening there was a service at St Laurence's followed by a procession in two columns with bands and banners. The evening was overshadowed by the death of Crimean War veteran, James Hoare of 27 Howard Street, who had a heart attack prior to the start while waiting to join the march.

Although there was censorship, the papers carried news of German attacks on mainland Britain. Such reports were usually brief like the one on a Zeppelin raid in May. 'From a military point of view the Zeppelin raid at South-on-sea was as futile as previous raids in other parts of the country. There was, however, one death, and considerable damage was done to property.' Two other people were injured during the attack but this was not reported.

A similarly brief report appeared after a London raid. The jury at the inquest of the three killed in a Zeppelin raid gave the verdict that they had died from suffocation and burns caused by some agent of a hostile force.

Fortunately for Reading it never became a target for German air raids, but Corporal J. Pollard, of 77 Filey Road, serving with the Royal Berks in France, was slightly wounded by a bomb from a Zeppelin. However unlikely it was to happen, it did not mean that no precautions would be taken to prevent any such

Trooper Potts on his wedding day.

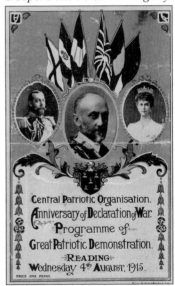

Programme of events to commemorate the first anniversary of the war. In the centre is the Mayor, Leonard Sutton.

The mayor and corporation leaving St Laurence's Church on Wednesday 4 August, after a service on the first anniversary of the war.

The Reading Chamber of Commerce War Hospitals Supplies Depot on Duke Street.

At the corner of Friar Street on 4 August 1915. A vast congregation joined in a solemn act of worship to commemorate the first anniversary of the war.

attack. The obvious precaution was a reduction in street and shop-lighting. Like it or not, it was law, and there was nothing anyone could do about it unless they wanted to pay a fine. One letter told fellow readers it was a necessary inconvenience: 'The edict having gone forth that the hitherto well-lighted streets of Reading must present an appearance less likely to attract the attention of hostile airmen, both public and authorities have complied with the new regulations in a manner which has ensured a gloom of the approved kind. It is not pleasant, but it is believed to be necessary, and therefore, it is no use wasting time and energy on futile grumblings.' However, 'if we avoid a problematic aerial danger but create a new one there is little advantage to us.'

Wokingham blacked out the top of its street lights in response to the new regulations, while Reading extinguished every other street lamp and restricted the lighting permitted. Shortly after the reduction in lighting, there was a fatal accident at the junction of King's and Queen's Road. In the dark, a woman was knocked down by a car. Later in the year, new lighting orders reduced street lighting further, with no naked lights in shops and no illuminations visible from the pavement.

Sons of Mr. and Mrs. A. EDGINGTON, Bulmershe Park, Woodley.

Bdr. E. EDGINGTON, R.G.A.—Wounded. Sergt. S. EDGINGTON, Royal Flying Corps. L.-Cpl. H. EDGINGTON, Military Mounted Police. Pte. W. EDGINGTON, Royal Berks Regt.

A Woodley family.

In modern parlance, it was a 'Catch 22' situation. Showing lights and lacking lights were both offences. Frank Payton, of 16 Auckland Road, pleaded guilty and was fined 5s for riding a bicycle without a light on Church Road.

Air raids, likely or not, provided insurance companies with new business. One of the first to advertise this new form of protection was the Hearts of Oak Assurance Company based in Brisbane Road. It invited clients to apply for insurance rates against aircraft raids. The darkened streets also increased the risk of accident. To protect against this, the London Guarantee & Accident Co., of Lincoln's Fields, provided a special policy providing 'substantial benefits at a moderate premium for personal injury sustained in the streets (at any time of the day or night), including accidents to or caused by vehicles'.

Annual Premium			
	5s	10s	20s
Death	£250	£500	£1000
Loss of 2 limbs, or 2 eyes or one limb and one eye	£250	£500	£1000
Loss of one limb or one eye	£125	£250	£500
Temporary total disablement, weekly allowance limited to 13 weeks	25s	£2 10s	£5

Although there were no civilian casualties caused by enemy action in Berkshire, it did not mean that everyone was safe. Moving into a war zone, even as a civilian, could have fatal consequences. The population read the news of the sinking of the *Lusitania* on 27 April, but one local family had a fatal connection with it. The niece of the secretary of Welford Park Club, to the west of Reading, was a passenger on the liner. Mrs Adams and her young son were travelling back to England to spend time with her husband, serving with the Canadian Army, before he went to France. They were both rescued but the child was dead. Naturally, 'the dastardly action of the Germans in torpedoing the *Lusitania* was strongly condemned from many pulpits' across Reading.

Even with news of great battles and casualties, concerns over Zeppelin raids and rising prices, life continued much as it had done in recent years. The papers carried articles about Reading F.C., who at the end of February were first equal with West Ham in the Southern League, the Fire Brigade supper at Englefield and whist drives in Mortimer. Reading Cricket Club announced its summer results at its AGM. *The Grip of Iron*, a French drama, playing at the County Theatre, was reviewed and Reverend Caulfield, although summoned, did not appear at his court case for riding a bicycle on a footpath. In his absence he was fined 6d with costs of 5s 6d.

Reading F.C. was part of the town's fabric, and the papers regularly carried lengthy details of the club's performance and position in the league. A month after being in first position, they dropped to fourth place and in the South-eastern League they were not doing well at all, being 15/21. Some of the players had joined the army and sent letters back to the paper or their local friends who shared the news with the papers. Soccer at the front was an important part of life.

Dickenson, the Reading half-back, wrote to the club secretary about his recent game: 'We are still resting and getting fairly good weather, so we indulge in the good old game. We are resting in a large town, and have a beautiful ground to play on, and a nice stand and good accommodation. We played the Glasgow Highlanders in the first round of the Divisional Shield, and, sorry to say, we suffered defeat 1 – 0. They were at a great advantage, for they were practically in football order, and we were in our every-day attire. The play was of a good standard as they had seven professionals in the team and we had six. The game caused great excitement amongst the many spectators.'

Like most of the men on active service, they did not want to stay there: 'I should love to come home now; I think I have done my bit… but I don't think it will be this season.' He was not to return, being killed in action on 28 May near La Bassée. Just fifteen days previously, another Reading player had been killed. Corporal Albert (Ben) Butler of the Footballers Battalion, Middlesex Regiment, a married man with a family, died of wounds received on the Somme on 13th May. A shell blew one leg off and the other was damaged by shrapnel. His brother was the landlord of the Star Inn, Caversham.

Of the men of Reading F.C. who enlisted, four were killed: Ben Butler, Joe Dickenson, Alan Foster and H.P. Shulto. The others returned home, but not always in one piece. Sergeant Blacktin, DCM, had part of his right hand blown off, all the more unfortunate as he was a violin player. Joe Bailey served with particular distinction with the

The Mayor and Corporate head the anniversary procession.

Even with a front-line life expectancy of around six weeks, junior officers still got married before they left for the front. This is Lieutenant C.E.B. Rogers of 7 Royal Berks and his bride Janie Pike of St Clair, Reading. He survived the war.

Footballers' Battalion. He was decorated three times for bravery, winning the DSO and MC with bar.

For many soldiers, the war was a time to reflect on God, especially just before leaving for Active Service. At Chelmsford Cathedral, the Chaplain-General confirmed soldiers from the 1st/4th Battalion, amongst others from the South Midland Division. Shaking their hands, he asked them to read a few verses of God's word every day and to live a Christian life. He told them 'they were going forth to their life – it might be going forth to their death, but there was no death to those who were in Christ Jesus.' In St Laurence's Church in Reading, the Bishop of Oxford confirmed five men of 7 Battalion and three of the Berkshire Yeomanry.

Adverts for days out continued. The GWR advertised trips to Cheltenham Steeplechases with a convenient train to the racecourse at ordinary, first and third class fares. Leaving Reading at 9.51 it would return at 5.00 pm, stopping at Tilehurst, Pangbourne, Goring, Cholsey, Wallingford and Didcot on the way.

For those unable to get away, there was always the circus. Lord John Sanger's Royal Circus and Menagerie was visiting Reading on Easter Monday. The stars were Russian Cossacks who leapt from one horse to another, and who, hanging from one stirrup, were dragged along the floor to escape detection. And of course there was always shopping. The Heelas Show Week started on Easter Tuesday, 6 April, with the new season's goods all over the store, including the 'latest arrivals in fashions, especially inexpensive copies of famous models'.

How things have changed. An event held at Reading F.C.'s military and patriotic fete on Whit Monday, in brilliant weather, in Prospect Park would certainly not be put on today. The grounds were crowded throughout the afternoon and evening by spectators eager to watch the sports such as boxing, whippet racing, musical chairs, tug-of-war, tilting at the bucket, five-a-side football in sacks – which caused much amusement – and the bun and bottle race. There were the usual ever-popular roundabouts, coconut shies and a Punch and Judy show with music provided by the Reading Temperance Band for the sports and dancing later in the evening. Naturally with so many people gathered in one place it was ideal for a recruitment meeting. For many the highlight was a Belgian game – 'Beheading the Cock'. For a fee the competitor had their head encased in a black sac and was given a sword. After finding the cock they had one swipe to decapitate the bird. The majority of competitors were soldiers showing off their military skill. Most got nowhere near the bird and one waved his sword over the crowd. The winner is unknown but his method was described by the *Chronicle*. Although his head was covered and he was taken away from the bird, he simply 'marched straight up to it, felt for it, found it, and then with a straight two-handed blow completely severed the cock's neck, to the great delight of the people'.

The *Chronicle* suggested something more in touch with the times for those who were not interested in going far or not interested in the latest fashion. The 96 Field Company, RE, stationed in Wargrave, were learning the skills they needed for the front. They had constructed 'a series of most elaborate trenches which are worthy of a visit. There are "dug-outs", gun emplacements, mining excavations…and give one a most vivid impression of the topics described in the newspapers'.

There was always local sport to watch and report. The Berkshire Bowls team was beaten by the Gloucestershire county team. More locally, summer brought out the cricket teams. It was a thriving sport at the biscuit factory even with so many men serving with the colours. The south beat the north in a very close match, 115 to 112, Sorting 'A' beat the tin shops 56 to 33, while Export lost to Continental 50 to 54. Further afield in Egypt, the Berkshire Yeomanry team was trounced by the Dorset Yeomanry, 123 to 245.

As usual in a British summer, 'unfavourable weather conditions interfered with the 42nd Woodley and Sonning Horticultural Show held in Woodley Recreation Ground. Attendance was down as were the number of exhibitors but this was due to them being in His Majesty's Forces. After judging had taken place, a gust of wind during a rainstorm blew the tent down containing fruit, needlework, eggs, jam, etc., and a display of sweet peas.' The quality of the exhibits was judged to be above average with T. Johnson growing the best white kidney potatoes, celery, cabbage lettuce, long white marrow, long green marrow, turnip, short carrots, shallots, red cabbage and garden cabbage. He gained forty-seven points, but was narrowly beaten by J. Reed, who was awarded forty-nine points for his fruit and flowers.

War snippets regularly included news on concert parties for troops and military weddings, such as that of Captain Frank Gilson of the Hampshire RHA to Adelaide Eustace. Crowthorne decided to form a

Home Defence Corps with seventy-three signing at the first meeting. Closer to Reading, the well-established Earley Defence Force was poised to open its new shooting range with Mr Joel chosen to both open the pavilion and fire the first shot. At the other side of the world, Howard Arle, of St Stephen's Church, was serving on HMS *Cadmus* during the Singapore mutiny. In France, Corporal Attwell had the dubious honour of being the first Tramway Department employee to be killed out of the 200 serving with the colours. There was a brief mention of a Reading taxi driver who had possibly died. On the Aisne, an ASC soldier had found a Reading taxi cab driver's metal badge. It was returned to Reading by the Metropolitan Police. It had been issued to William Brooks of 24 St John's Road, employed by Mr Hindle of Tilehurst Road.

For Kitchener's men billeted in and around Reading, boxing was popular entertainment with regular tournaments taking place, some for big prize money. One was particularly noteworthy: 'Of the many entertainments arranged for the soldiers of the Berkshire Regiment stationed in and around Reading, none has aroused such genuine enthusiasm or given such enjoyment to the men as the boxing tournament which took place in the Large Town Hall on Friday evening' (29 January). 'The big event was a good ten-round contest for a purse of £6 between Private Evans (8 Battalion) and Private Spiers

Sergeant Alfred Ayres, 2nd Battalion Royal Berks, whose home was in King's Road Caversham, with his bride, Lilian Johnson of King's Meadow Road. The photo was taken after the wedding ceremony at London Street Primitive Methodist Church. Lilian was employed at the Palace Theatre. Sergeant Ayres was training recruits in Portsmouth where they went after the wedding.

Men of the 7th and 8th battalions of the Royal Berkshire Regiment enjoying a supper on 9 April in the Trinity Congregational Schoolroom.

(7 Battalion).' They were so evenly matched that the judges couldn't decide on the winner, so the referee did. Not all fights were of the same quality. In the final of the 11-stone fight, Driver Rushton of the RFA beat Private Ellis of 7 Battalion, who gave up in the first round.

Kitchener was a national hero. In response to his call for volunteers, Reading had raised four battalions for his New Army. Showing his admiration for the great man, reservist Gunner H. Gould, and his wife, of 31 Sherman Street, decided to name their son after him; they christened him Kitchener Gould.

Although Kitchener did not visit Reading, other people of influence did. Two well-known figures visited during the year. Hilaire Belloc spoke at the Town Hall about the war and Lord French addressed troops. The Berkshire Volunteer Regiment paraded in front of Reading Station for inspection by Lord French, former commander of the BEF. He was travelling the GWR line inspecting contingents of volunteers. In his thirty-minute break he addressed them, suggesting that instead of their short-term contract they should all sign on for the duration.

Family cult status continued in 1915. In February, Mrs Wheeler of 1 Beecham Road was congratulated on having five sons and two sons-

Reading Athletes' Volunteer Force, E and F companies, about to defend Tilehurst Waterworks against an enemy force made up from A,B and C companies.

The opening ceremony for the two rifle ranges in Sol Joel Park.

Men of the Berkshire Volunteers march through town during the anniversary parade on 4 August 1915.

Men of either the 7th or 8th Battalion leaving Reading station for Salisbury Plain and further training.

Officers of 8 Battalion pose for a group photo before they left Reading for Salisbury Plain.

in-law serving in the army. James, a Lance-Corporal in the RSF, had recently returned from the front with rheumatism; Fred and Harry were Privates in 9 Battalion at Portsmouth; Charles was with the 2nd/4th Battalion at Chelmsford and Leonard was serving at Northampton with the 4th Reserve Battalion. Her two sons-in-law, Sergeant J. Andrews and Private B. Hester, were with 6 Battalion at Colchester, and 2nd/4th Battalion at Chelmsford respectively.

Throughout the war, readers were kept informed about the military career of their MP, Captain (later Colonel) Leslie Wilson, through his letters. The thirty-nine-year-old territorial soldier had fought in the South African war where he had been awarded the DSO and been Mentioned in Dispatches. Originally serving in the Royal Marine Light Infantry, he had become a gunner with the Berkshire RHA and in March was promoted to command Hawke Battalion in the Royal Naval Division prior to their leaving for Gallipoli.

Another important local figure was mentioned during September. Lord Reading who lived at Foxhill House in Earley was in America acting on behalf of the government. Readers were informed that 'German sympathisers in America are conducting a virulent campaign against the loan to the Allies, and the lives of the members of the British Commission, which includes Lord Reading, have been threatened by letter. The members of the commission do not disclose their plans, and go alone into the public thoroughfares, followed by one or more detectives.'

Food was becoming an issue for many people. Increasing prices were affecting living standards. Fish prices at Billingsgate were between twenty-five and fifty per cent higher than in the previous year, with supply at about half of 1914. The prices being fetched for fat-stock were also exceedingly high. Bread was essential and bakers were punished for selling underweight loaves, an offence that was taken seriously by the courts. The reason: a loaf one ounce less than the correct weight would rob a labourer, buying an average of four loaves a day a full loaf in just eight days.

The *Chronicle* compared food prices before the war and towards the end of January 1915.

Cost of food		
Food	Before the war	January 1915
4lb. loaf	6½d	7½d
7lb. best household flour	11½d	1s 2½d
English butter a 1lb.	1s 7d	1s 7d
English Cheddar a 1lb	10½d	1s 0d
Sirloin – whole a 1lb.	1s 0d	1s 0d
New Zealand leg of lamb a a lb.	8½d	9d
Pork loin a lb.	10½d	10½d
Danish bacon (side) a lb.	9½d	11½d
Tea – Stores mixture a lb.	1s 7d	1s 10d
Granulated sugar per 1lb.	2d	3½d
Eggs – dozen newly laid	1s 6d	2s 6d
Potatoes (for 14,16 or 18lb.)	1s 0d	1s 0d
Cooking onions a lb.	2d	2d

Bread Down! The result of an axle breaking during delivery. No one was hurt.

One big decision was made by the Reading Workhouse Board of Governors that would save money in this time of financial constraint: inmates should have margarine instead of butter.

There were also worries about the manpower available for the next harvest, a harvest that was expected to be a good one, even bountiful in some districts. A wet July had been good for the crops and the Board of Agriculture predicted most foodstuffs at close to 1914 levels.

While the harvest was related to rural Berkshire, it is important to remember that Reading Borough was a centre for the transport and slaughter of livestock, and many other crops, as well as producing them. The 1915 agricultural analysis showed that Reading had 40,185 acres under crops and grass: 10,132 of corn, 3,108 of root and potato, 5,657 of other crops, 18,897 of arable land and 21,288 of permanent grass. There were also large numbers of animals: 1,709 horses, 4,000 cows and heifers, 3,277 other cattle, 2,477 pigs and 10,052 sheep.

Mention was made of the driving of bullocks on a Sunday. Animals were regularly moved through the town to the station or the abattoir. Their movement was not always peaceful. In late August, a runaway bull in Prospect Street knocked down workhouse inmate William Salmon who was attempting to stop it. The bull was taken into a stable and two drovers came to take it for slaughter. As soon as the door was opened, it escaped, running in the direction of Calcot. Two weeks later, a cow found its way into Messrs E.J. Jackson's shop in London Road. Having made its way into the cellar, it was only with some difficulty that it was eventually persuaded to leave.

A Help in the Harvest Fields appeal was made by the Bishop of Oxford as one way of dealing with the manpower shortage. He asked the well-to-do to help in the fields over the summer. Another idea was to use children. It was suggested that schooling was secondary to the nation's needs: 'In view of the shortage of farm labour it is desirable that boys of twelve years and upwards should be allowed to work on farms during the period of the war, such work to count as school attendance.'

This would help solve another shortage. Not only did farming, industry and mining suffer because of the numbers volunteering for active service, but education was also affected. By the middle of 1915, half of all the male teachers in Berkshire were in the services, and any replacements available were women.

Many teachers became officers and some were decorated for their bravery. Owen Attewell, master at Welford Village School, volunteered in August 1915, was a sergeant by October and commissioned in 1916. By 1917 he was a major, subsequently winning an MC and bar. After the war, he returned to teaching.

There was also an increase in the number of children truanting. The parents of those who continually missed school, just as today, faced prosecution. At the start of November, three families appeared in front of the Bench for not sending their children to school. Henry Roberts, of 3 Recreation Road, Tilehurst, was fined £1 or fourteen days' in default, William Creed, of 9 Kew Terrace, Tilehurst, was fined 10s or seven days' default, and Charles Simpson, of 16 Commercial Hall, Coley Place, was also fined 10s or seven days' default.

Another shortage that was having an important effect was dye for clothing. Germany had been the main European producer of dyestuffs. The writer warned that this shortage would mean that nearly everything would be grey, with some, very few, browns and blues. There would also be no change of style because factories were concentrating on army uniform production. Supply was going to be considerably less than demand and there was no left-over stock from last autumn as the army had bought it up for the New Armies. Emphasising the predicted shortage, it was suggested that any slack would be taken up by discharged soldiers' suits and that some manufacturers were already out of suits and overcoats at popular prices. To the wealthy, of course, this was of no importance.

A shortage of coal was predicted and, as every year, people were urged to stock up in the summer when demand was lower. Fortunately there was an alternative – peat. Stevens & Co. often advertised on the front page using the military or political situation to make a point about the need to buy their coal. Their 5 November advert was a poem about the war situation:

The Zeppelin has its terrors and the submarine's a scare
And other dangers threaten us by land and sea and air.
But 'K' is on the warpath and 'J' is on the blue
And we've got to face the Teuton and a coal-less winter too.
So be cheery and light hearted, we shall get our flour and meat
And if so be that we can't get coal, well – 'Stevens' will give us
peat.

Come frost – come snow – with miners slow, it won't fill us with
distress
There's abundance of peat, which gives plenty of heat, and this is
the address
Stevens & Co., 3 Broad Street, Reading.
Price 11s 6d per load (equal in bulk to 13 cwts. of coal).

When coal was available, it was not consistently priced. The price of
standard house coal ranged from 30 to 36s a ton or in small quantities
from 1s 7d to 1s 10d a cwt. In London, the Board of Trade had arranged
with major suppliers to limit cost. As a result it was cheaper than in
Reading. Surely, if Reading merchants charged more, then London
merchants would compete for business. The Reading Finance
Committee were satisfied that the prices charged were reasonable and
that no limitation of profits was necessary.

That able-bodied men were at a premium was noted by one writer
who suggested that women were a perfectly logical substitute in many
jobs and that only simple prejudice was stopping this from happening.

*A photo of Reading's first tram conductresses. They were paid at the same rate as
the men.*

He pointed his finger at the Council: 'It is surely time that the Reading Tramways Committee decided to put any prejudice which may exist aside and appoint women conductors on the electric cars to fill the places of men who enlist. When the country needs all the men it can obtain for active service or the making of munitions, the duties of tramway conducting may surely be placed in the hands of others than able-bodied males.' He then pointed out that this had already happened in many large towns and that in some towns, women had been engaged as bus conductors, far more awkward work than fare collection on a tram. He also castigated the Council for wanting to move men from council departments to the tramways: 'If there are any able-bodied men who can be spared from any department, they ought to be placed at the disposal of the country.' The Tramways Committee took no notice.

Not all companies were so entrenched. The grocery chain, International Stores, in a 1916 advert proudly noted that, although nearly 2,000 of their men were in the army, there was no problem with service. Their answer to the shortage of men was to employ women. They told Reading newspaper readers that they had an able and willing staff of lady grocers ready to attend to them who had untiring energy, adaptability, and strong will.

Another new bus route from Reading to Streatley and Reading to Maidenhead. There was still considerable demand for travel.

Prices rose faster than wages throughout the war. This naturally caused industrial tension. Most companies realised this and gave their workers' pay rises, some quicker than others, some at better rates. Two Reading companies were pro-active in their approach. Huntley & Palmers gave their workers a war bonus and Simonds gave their employees an increased salary. The Huntley & Palmers bonus was across the board – 2s a week for everyone. At Simonds it was graduated: lads earning 16s or less received 1s; lads and men earning between 16s and 40s received a 2s rise.

Suddenly, orders for military supplies were increasing. Huntley & Palmers were prospering and employees went on full time at the start of March. As a result, the men received a 2s war bonus in addition to their weekly wage. The three-quarter time had lasted only a week, and the men were not out of pocket, as they had received a 4s bonus. Reading Town Council increased the wages of some of its employees. Because of the shortage of labour, it was decided to give 3s a week increase to workers at Manor Farm at a cost of £500 a year. This was in response to a petition by fifty-two workmen claiming that the cost of living had increased by twenty-five per cent.

Across the country, prosperity increased. At the end of January 1915 there were 637,361 paupers in England and Wales, 17.1 persons per thousand. The figure was 17.5 for the corresponding month in 1914. The 1915 figure was the smallest since records began in 1875.

KING'S CONGRATULATIONS.

Mr. THOMAS ARCHER, who has completed fifty years' continuous service with Huntley & Palmers, Ltd., has five sons serving with H.M. Forces, and the King has sent him a letter congratulating him upon this fact.

Mr. THOS. ARCHER.

Pte. STANLEY A. ARCHER, 3rd Batt. Grenadier Guards.

Farrier-Corpl. SIDNEY J. ARCHER, A.S.C.— Invalided home with rheumatism.

Gunner EDWARD C. ARCHER, Berks R.H.A.

Pte. ERNEST A. ARCHER, 3rd. Batt. Royal Berks Regt.

Q.M.S. THOMAS H. ARCHER, South Wales Borderers.

Fifty years continuous employment with Huntley & Palmers was quite an achievement as was having five sons serving with the colours.

In a story that prefigures modern times, Reading's increased prosperity was shown as today by higher house prices. By the end of the year small houses were at a premium: 'From a period of slump and depression there has been a recovery by leaps and bounds, until now the empty houses of Reading are almost full, especially those of the cottage and villa classes, which are most difficult to obtain.' The reason then, as now, was that 'Reading is in a prosperous way just now. Employment is abundant and wages are good, whilst the families of those who are out "doing their bit" for their country are in receipt of allowances which, in many instances, make them better off than they were before the war.' Again, as now, there was a shortage of houses and insufficient building. This resulted in rising rents and property owners 'reaping a fair return for their money'.

While the above suggests that Reading in general was a prosperous town, this was not true for everyone. There were still many poor families, and with Christmas on the horizon, the Reading Philanthropic Institution asked for help. In 1915 they had collected over 1800 articles of clothing, boots and shoes, along with a large quantity of books, games and toys. This allowed them 'to provide 310 parcels to the deserving poor of Reading'. This year they appealed for more of the

In August, a plane piloted by an army officer alighted in a field of stubble in Coley. It ran into a hedge, fell into the road turning turtle in the process. The plane was wrecked but the pilot unhurt.

PARCELS TO PRISONERS OF WAR
AND THE
TROOPS AT HOME & ABROAD.

Send for Special List compiled with a view to
facilitating the selection of Goods for despatch to
the Expeditionary Forces in various countries,
also Home Forces, and Prisoners of War.

One of the large Daily Consignments sent from our Store.

You send us the Order   We do the rest.

GREGORY, LOVE & CO., LTD.,
THE STORES, READING.

Wherever they were, a parcel from home was always welcome and profitable for the company sending it.

same as they had 'a great number of poor families on their book who they hoped to assist by food and clothes at Christmas time'.

Thinking of Christmas, the Master of Reading Workhouse proposed there should be no beer on Christmas Day. Although this would have saved money, the resolution was not approved. Although the king had abstained, the committee took a broader look at the members of government and what was drunk at the Guildhall banquet. A resolution that beer be provided was carried thirteen to eight.

Pupils at George Palmer School making the wooden parts of cradles and splints. This was a voluntary activity undertaken after school on Wednesday and on Saturday morning.

Attendance was low at George Palmer School because of a measles outbreak, but this did not stop the children enjoying the end of term. As in the previous year, ordinary work was suspended in the afternoon of the last day and this time for a visit from Father Christmas. He arrived in a car 'about 2.30 p.m. and gained admittance to the school through an open window, heavily laden with a sack of toys. The joy of the children was intense. They sang and danced to their hearts' content and finally received a tiny gift.'

Frank Page, Pawnbroker and Jeweller of 79 King's Road, was also thinking of Christmas with his war-themed advertisement: 'Another raid in King's Road. Not of the Zeppelin type, embracing every description of diamond, gem, wedding, keeper and signet rings, gold and silver wrist watches, gold and silver Alberts, gold bracelets and necklets...bronzed figures...a large stock of men's new and second-hand suits...a visit will convince of a saving of 30 per cent.'

In early December, the voluntary Lord Derby scheme closed. The concept behind the scheme was that men who 'voluntarily registered their name would be called upon for service only when necessary'. Married men had an added incentive in that they were advised they would be called up only once the supply of single men was exhausted. The scheme was also referred to as the Group System as men were classified in groups according to their year of birth and marital status and were to be called up with their group when it was required...215,000 men enlisted while the scheme was operational, and another 2,185,000 attested for later enlistment. However, 38 per cent of single men and 54 per cent of married men who were not in "starred" occupations failed to come forward. Those

Corporal Howard had his photo taken before he left for France. He served with 6 Royal Berks and returned home at the end of the war.

enlisted under this scheme wore a khaki armband with a red crown with issue commencing on 20 December at the Town Hall. It was superseded by the Military Service Act 1916 which introduced conscription.

Just before Christmas the Reading Parliamentary Recruiting Committee made a final appeal to the young men of Reading: 'Voluntary enlistment ends on 11 December. There can only be two replies to the nation's call "willing" or "unwilling". It is better to enrol as a volunteer than to run the risk of being "conscripted".' After that date there would be no deferment, only immediate service. 'The group system with its deferred service, its 14 days' notice before being called up, and its right of appeal on personal or business grounds, is only for those who enlist before 11 December.'

In this final appeal to get every available man to attest under the Group System shame was used: 'Let him join the Army ...and show his country that he puts her interests before his own' and more strongly 'the "stand-backs" will form for the rest of their lives a "group" to which lasting stigma will attach.' Even this did not get every suitable man into the forces.

A further war-time inconvenience started during December, one that

Christmas at Heelas'. An advert with the emphasis on children and a request to help the sick and wounded.

continued well after the war had finished. The Reading banks placed an advert in the papers telling customers of a change in banking hours. On and after Monday, 13 December, they would close to the public at 3.00 pm, except on a Wednesday when they closed at 12.30 pm as usual.

War or no war, it would be business as usual for Reading's stores: 'A second Christmas finds us still in the throes of war, and therefore the joyous festivals of Christmastide will be shorn of some of its old glamour. Whilst our "Tommies" are fighting their country's battles abroad, suffering without demur the hardships of the trenches, those at home will hardly be in festive spirit. Nevertheless, in a quiet way Christmas will be observed, and there are two aspects of it that will serve to command attention. There will be a general desire to remember the soldiers, and, secondly, the children will not be forgotten. What can be done for them in the circumstances will be done.' It was also observed that the Christmas trade 'far exceeded expectations; and on Christmas Eve Reading presented as busy a spectacle as it had ever done. For the nonce people seemed to have forgotten the war.'

Whilst full of pathos, the bottom line of this was money: 'In order to meet the Christmas rush, the Reading Early Closing Association has arranged that Reading shops will be open all day on Wednesday, December 22, and shops will be closed Christmas Day (Saturday) and the following Monday (Boxing Day) and Tuesday.'

Eager to join in the rush, Hill's Rubber Co. advertised its wares in a similar vein: 'This is a utilitarian age, and especially at the present time it is necessary that money should be wisely spent and not frittered away.' Making the sales really topical, they were 'selling goods suitable for wounded soldiers, hot water bottles, air pillows and cushions for relief, rubber pads for sticks and crutches. Rubber overshoes and boots for nurses who go out in all weathers. For the little ones, unbreakable dolls and animals and rubber funniosities such as "dying Kaisers", pigs, monkeys, flying sausages, glum faces, balloons and plate-lifters.'

To aid husbands with their Christmas shopping, Hedgecocks of Broad Street had some useful suggestions: 'Furs are always acceptable. We cannot all give diamonds for Christmas gifts, but a set of really nice furs is within reach of the most modest purse – at least, it is at Hedgecocks. The furs that are now in fashion are not expensive when you consider that fashionable sets are priced from 21s and upwards to, say, £8.8.0d, it is evident that a gift of furs will fit with whatever you wish to spend. Squirrel, Red and Black Fox, handsome black wolf, Coney and Musquash furs are all well represented at Hedgecocks.' For those on a lower budget, there was a great range of imitation sets from 4s 11d to 19s 11d the set, and of course the Christmas staples of gloves, scarves and handkerchiefs.

Colebrook & Co. were pleased to let their customers know they had secured supplies for the Christmas trade, equal in quality to former years. While proud to record that over 100 of their employees were serving and that many more had attested, it had not been possible to replace them. With a greatly reduced staff they earnestly requested the placing of orders for Christmas fare as early as possible so they could 'give all possible attention to their valued orders'.

Patriotism and emulation were suitable ways of getting money from deep pockets. A £25 donation by the king to the Weekly Dispatch Tobacco Fund was the start of yet another request for money for 'smokes' to show Reading's gratitude and admiration for the county regiment. Advance warning of a street collection was given: 'On 1 January, money would be raised by the sale of Snowdrops (emblem of hope),' made by Mr. Groom's cripple children and others and badges. Half would be donated to Royal Berks PoWs, ten per cent to county and borough police who were PoWs and the remainder to the PoW Central Fund.

By showing how much they had achieved, the War Hospital Supplies Depot attempted to solicit contributions to keep their work going. In the short period from 20 October to 10 December, they had dispatched: 'blankets 3, cloths 69, gloves 18, hankies 282, mufflers 55, pillows 26, pneumonia jackets 72, bed sheets (pairs) 44, shirts 115, slippers (pairs) 125, socks (pairs) 135, splint fasteners 70, swabs 1248, towels 29, treasure bags 103, Turkish towelling swabs 140, vests 216, bed rests 39, crutches (pairs) 206, leg rests 234, tables 72, trays 50, walking-sticks 20, also thousands of splints, bandages, etc.' The sum of £505 was subscribed and over 1000 voluntary workers of both sexes and all ages were kept busy making additional similar and other articles. To keep them supplied required money. Donations (large or small) were gratefully accepted.

The Christmas rush referred to the Post Office as well as the shops. With so many postmen with the colours, between 200 and 300 women were employed for sorting and delivering in Reading and county. The management were proud that 'there was not a single failure or hitch of any kind, and not a mail was missed. A record for Reading having been established in regard to the hours of delivery and completion of deliveries on Christmas Day.' Women who would not normally deliver the mail did a better job than the missing men folk had previously done.

Readers were warned of a change coming in with the New Year. From 10 January 'all external lamps, flares, and fixed lights of all descriptions, whether public or private, must be extinguished except

Female volunteers working in the sewing room at the War Supplies Depot in Duke Street.

The splint room at the War Supplies Depot.

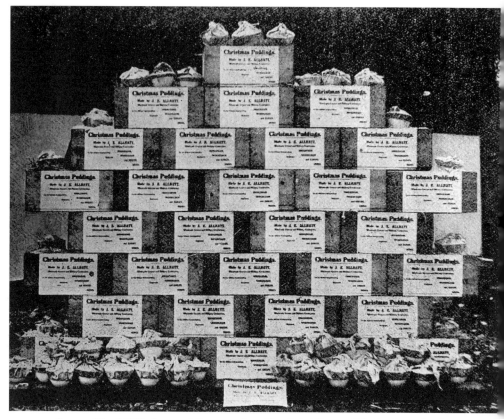

Some of the 1,000 plum puddings produced by J.E. Allnatt of Sindlesham, for the British Army. Each weighed four pounds and was despatched to Berkshire Regiment troops at home and abroad.

public lamps and other lamps' necessary for safety. Any un-extinguished light had to be reduced to the minimum intensity for safety. In all premises, internal lights had to be shaded so that no more than a dull light was visible from any direction outside. Lighting-up times for vehicles would be thirty minutes after sunset and all vehicles would carry a red light on the off-side rear.

In the Christmas Eve edition of the *Chronicle*, a writer summed up the year for Reading: 'The year 1915 as affecting Reading and the county has been envisaged in aspects of war. It is impossible that it could be otherwise, in face of such a colossal and terrible struggle. The record of the year's local events has thus been chiefly to do, directly or indirectly, with the influence of the war. It has been a year of

A ward decorated for Christmas at Wilson School War hospital.

Christmas in Battle Hospital.

remarkable activity, alike in regard to the raising of recruits for the Berkshires and other units and of remedial measures for the brave fellows who have sacrificed so much for their country. Looking back one can say that the record of Reading and the county in these directions during the year is not one as to which Berkshire need be ashamed.'

The weather also left its mark on 1915. There were severe gales on Boxing Day that caused much destruction in the form of blown-down fences, slates and trees. A Reading taxi-cab driver and his fare had a lucky escape outside the Royal Berkshire Hospital. Miss Weeks, from London, was visiting the hospital and on arrival got out on London Road. The driver also alighted and, as she was paying him, a warning voice shouted and the driver looked up to see a tree falling. Quickly he 'drew the lady out of danger' and the tree crashed down on to the taxi, wrecking it and blocking the road, holding up traffic for a considerable time.

CHAPTER 3

1916
The Realization

The *Reading Standard* editorial summarised 1915 in its first edition of the New Year: 'The war has cast its shadow over all public and private activities during the year, affecting in innumerable ways our corporate and individual life. Few indeed are the families that have not one or more members in the Army or Navy, many of whom, alas! have laid down their lives for their country. In sending recruits to the forces Berkshire has done splendidly...the response to Lord Derby's appeal for recruits has been highly satisfactory, and the authorities were almost overwhelmed with the rush of men wishing to attest. Reading is also doing its part in the manufacture of munitions, and so flourishing is the trade of the town that the National Relief Fund has very few beneficiaries. So far from unemployment being rife at this time of the year, the scarcity of labour constitutes a serious problem, and women have replaced men in many occupations.' This was not the case at Reading Council who would be criticised for their backward attitudes later in the war.

Miss Hussey, the first female conductor of the annual children's concerts.

A more positive attitude was shown by the organisers of the

The Sutherlands on Christchurch Road became an auxiliary hospital in 1916. It was opened by Mrs Benyon, lady president of the Berkshire branch of the British Red Cross, and wife of the Lord Lieutenant.

Children's Concerts whose conductor was with the colours. Innovatively they held a Wednesday afternoon matinee as well as the usual performances and 'for the first time in twenty-five years a lady wielded the baton'.

Bad weather saw the Old Year out and within days of the New Year, the *Chronicle* reported considerable damage to property by a storm: 'Not for many years has so much damage been done by a storm in Reading at one particular spot.' The area affected was Elm Park where the strong wind blew the roof off the Western Enclosure. Some of it fell in the road but most was carried by another gust over Norfolk Road where some fell in a garden, the remainder damaging the roofs of a number of properties. Four houses suffered damage: numbers 103, 105, 107 and 109 Norfolk Road. How destructive the wind was is shown by the damage to number 107: two chimney-stacks down; 230 slates smashed; three lengths of guttering broken; thirty ridge tiles broken; large portion of fence damaged; large hole in roof and ceiling of front bedroom. At number 105, Mrs Dummer had a lucky escape. She was in the garden at the time, and being partly deaf, did not hear her husband's warning to get in the house. If she had she would have been crushed to death. A six foot high pile of corrugated iron and timber landed a few inches in front of her. Although unharmed she was severely shaken.

The year 1916 was set to be darker than the previous year. In order to make sure citizens knew when vehicles needed to have lights on and when the town would be darkened a simple table was printed in the *Chronicle*, week by week.

Date	Vehicles to be lighted	Town to be darkened
January 10	4.40	5.40
January 11	4.42	5.42
January 12	4.43	5.43
January 13	4.44	5.44
January 14	4.45	5.45
January 15	4.46	5.46
January 16	4.48	5.48

There were concerns for safety, so guidance was provided. Pedestrians were urgently advised by the Hon. Sec. of the Berks Automobile Club, 'to walk in the path and not in the road as the amount of light allowed is insufficient to enable the driver to see a pedestrian at any appreciable distance, especially in country roads'. There were not always footpaths, in such areas the suggestion was that 'pedestrians should walk on their right side of the road so as to face the approaching traffic and avoid the risk of being overtaken by vehicles coming up from behind them'. It was pointed out that soldiers in uniform were particularly hard to see.

Naturally, insurance companies were quick to provide assistance. On the front page of 1 January edition, the *Reading Standard* carried a large advert for insurance headed 'Darkened streets increase the risk of accidents.' The London Guarantee and Accident Co. Ltd. offered a special policy, for moderate payment, to provide substantial benefits

The graphic Air Raid Distress Fund badge.

for personal injury sustained in the streets (at any time of day or night), including accidents to or caused by vehicles.

Linked with the darkness was the threat of the Zeppelin. Alderman Bull, Chairman of the Watch Committee, 'made an important statement in regard to the precautions to be taken in the event of a Zeppelin raid'. When the alarm sounded, 'everyone should get under cover, and…the lights in private houses, shops and every other description of buildings should be extinguished, and only candles be used; also that the gas should be turned off at the meter and the electric lights at the switches.'

Although there were no raids, there certainly were scares. After one incident, the *Chronicle* reported what it felt was both a humorous and nerve-wracking situation. It occurred at a time before most people had gone to bed and as a result some strange scenes were seen. Men left their games at the club unfinished and rushed off home. Tramcars dashed to the depot, leaving their erstwhile passengers to make their way home in the darkness. Business continued but by candlelight, to the great inconvenience of all. The worst hit were those travelling on the railway: 'For three-and-a-half hours…the passengers were confined to their lightless compartments.' The writer concluded by saying Reading should think itself lucky that the risk of a Zeppelin visit was extremely unlikely.

Showing a light at night was in contravention to the Lights Order of 1915. This was a regulation that was strictly enforced as many

Reading citizens found to their cost. Arthur Shepherd was one of many over the year to be fined for that offence. He pleaded guilty and, as it was his first offence, it was only a 10s fine. Later in the year, the offence resulted in heavier fines and even prison. In late October, George Fuller of 217 King's Road was fined £5 in respect to the inside lights at 209 London Road, and, for a similar offence, his second in eight days, Llewellyn Roberts, of 44 Orts Road, was sentenced to fourteen days.

Companies such as Suttons Seeds went to great lengths to make sure they did not contravene the restrictions. Over a six day period in January they had blinds put over all the windows, all the lights shaded and the shiny tiles in the potato warehouse painted. When this proved insufficient they had several ground floor office windows painted out and informed staff that they were personally responsible for any penalty imposed by the authorities.

Another sign of the times was the scaling back of postal deliveries. Tilehurst was hard hit by the shortage of postmen. As a result the mid-day delivery of letters was suspended, 'and also the 11.15 am and the 1.30 pm dispatches'. The wall boxes were now only being cleared twice a day, at 9 am and 7.15 pm.

Although Christmas was over, the Christmas Fete for Belgian Relief children was held on New Year's Day at St James' Schoolrooms. The eighty-four children were wished a Happy New Year by the mayor, provided with tea, treated to entertainments and given toys.

In the same week the mayor was able to bring cheer to another group in Reading. During August he had received a quantity of meat from the Queensland government for distribution amongst the distressed people of Reading. Whilst the meat was in storage at the Reading Ice Company, a committee of the National Relief Fund decided who should receive it, and how much.

A particularly sad funeral in Reading Cemetery was that of twenty-four-year-old Lieutenant William Rogers, RFC, of 65 Swainstone Road. He had been killed on 28 December while flying a Curtis aircraft at 150 foot when it nose-dived into the ground. Rogers was one of the many who returned from abroad to serve their homeland. Having emigrated to Canada, he had made a career out of motor-cycle racing in America. He was buried with full military honours.

By 1916, the people of Reading had become used to military

funerals for men, but not so much for women. On 4 October, Sister Alice Russell, who died in the Queen Alexandra's Hospital for sick sisters in London, was given a full military funeral. Her coffin was drawn on a gun-carriage, preceded by the band of the Royal Berks, to a service at King's Road Baptist Church. She was forty-two and the eldest daughter of Augustus Russell of 6 Fatherson Road. Before the war she had been a school nurse in London and had served with Queen Alexandra's Imperial Military Nursing Service in Malta from whence she was invalided home on 27 September.

The *Reading Standard* started the year with two different casualty lists in the same paper. One listed four Royal Berks soldiers killed, eight wounded, eight wounded and missing, and one dead, with one Berkshire Yeomanry soldier and one ASC man killed. Why there was a second list was not explained. This recorded a further one Berkshire Yeoman killed and ten wounded and, for the Royal Berks, listed five killed, one died of wounds, nine wounded, one wounded and missing, nine PoW and one missing, believed dead.

Mention has previously been made of PoW correspondence and the fact that some soldiers were under-age. The youngest to date was Private William Dunn of 1 Battalion. When a PoW in Meinster Camp, he wrote home that he was 'well but food is scarce, and warm clothes welcome, as the weather is very cold'. He was thankful for the parcels received, the paper stated, adding that he was only sixteen years and eight months old and that he was an only son.

In March, notice was drawn to another under-age soldier. Percy Harold Quarterman from Newbury was commissioned in the 3rd/23rd London Regiment at the age of seventeen. He was transferred to the 2nd/4th East Lancashire Regiment and was killed in action, aged nineteen, on 9 October 1917 during Third Ypres and buried in Tyne Cot cemetery.

Holyport was the scene of an attempted escape by PoWs. Leutnant Otto Thielen, who had been rescued from his downed aircraft in the North Sea, and naval Leutnant Hans Keilhary were sentenced to nine months at the Military Detention Barracks at Chelmsford. There was insufficient evidence to convict them of tunnelling from the bathroom, thirty-four feet under the main building, but they both pleaded guilty to sawing floorboards under a bed while other escapees played the mouth organ. Both had previously escaped from Donnington Hall in

September 1915. They had been recaptured in the Chatham district after a few days' liberty.

Studying the end of year report by the Chief Constable of Reading, indicating the level of crime in the town, the modern reader must wonder: would it be possible to categorise people in custody in this way today and what do these statistics tell us about crime? Since 1914 the total number of arrests was up by four to 354, but this did not include seventeen civil apprehensions. Of the arrested, 279 were employed, 151 married and 196 were borough residents. Seven could neither read nor write, 342 only imperfectly and 22 could read and write well. Considering the shortage of officers, the Chief Constable believed the force were doing a good job, ably assisted by the Special Constables.

Drunkenness was down again with ninety-four apprehended and four summoned. This was a decrease of fifteen compared with the previous twelve months. Fifty-eight of these cases were residents.

The report highlighted some of the other aspects of policing a large town. They had been responsible for billeting 6,236 officers, men, horses and vehicles. The number of enemy aliens registered before moving on was 138, the number arrested and taken to concentration camps or prison was twenty-one. Some 500 alien friends were also registered. Around 1,170 visits to pigeon lofts were made, 415 permits to keep homing pigeons issued and 253 licences to move pigeons were granted. They had received 9,462 letters and communications and sent out 23,679 letters, circulars and informations (sic). The Chief Constable had received thirty-one anonymous letters containing valuable information which could not be corroborated due to anonymity. They had arrested twenty-three people for other police forces as well as returning fifty-one lost children to their parents and putting nine horses, four cows and three sheep, found on the highways, in the pound.

Fortunately, there was still little in the way of serious crime. William Norris was summoned for keeping a dog without a licence and admitted the offence. Fred Higgins, a Clyde soldier, had obviously not read the papers. He was 'summoned for not keeping burning a lamp so contrived as to render easily distinguishable every letter and figure on the identification plate on a motor car in Alexandra Road.' He was lucky. The case was dismissed and he was ordered to pay costs. Another soldier fell foul of the law. Private John Symons was charged with attempted suicide on 10 January. He had been found on the floor in a doorway in Broad Street, shivering and with a very weak pulse. There was an open razor in his hand. On inspection he was found to have superficial cuts to his cheeks and neck. When questioned, he could not say who he was. He was discharged and handed over to the military.

The use of Reading Gaol changed during the year. In 1915 it had discharged 331 men, of whom thirty-six were soldiers returned to their units under escort, and eighty-six women back to civilian life. The remainder had been moved to prisons in Oxford, Shepton Mallet and Winchester. Their place was to be taken by alien prisoners interned for the war. One of these escaped in November 1916. Louis Claas, a Belgian with strong pro-German views, evaded capture for over a year and then returned to the prison. Now a soldier in the Middlesex Regiment, he had ostensibly come to collect some property he had left when he escaped. Needless to say he did not get in.

Bigamy was one crime that increased during the war. By the end of the war it had become classed by many judges as not being a serious offence in the cases of men who were soldiers. It took a ruling by Lord Reading to reverse this attitude. A typical case was that of Bessie Janice Dance of 10 Blagrave Buildings who was charged with bigamously marrying Thomas Jones on 18 January while married to Arthur Dance, a serving soldier. Jones was charged with aiding, abetting, counselling and procuring Dance to commit the offence. Jones was billeted on them in Slough just before her husband enlisted. Returning home on leave, he found his child gone and the house empty. He had received letters from her while in hospital wounded but did not suspect Jones. Dance was given a four month sentence and Jones seven.

A reduction in business hours was discussed at the start of the year. With little business being done after 6.00 pm, the large drapery establishments in the town centre decided that all would close at that time for a month. Naturally there was no consensus. The manager of Messrs Farrer and Sons, newsagents and stationers in Broad Street, disagreed. He found little change in trade because the public purchased books and magazines to read at home during the evenings, while Mr J.C. Gilkes, owner of a toy, fancy and stationery business in Broad Street, favoured all year round closing at 7.00 pm. Reading and District

Grocers' Association favoured early closing on Monday, Tuesday and Thursday at 6.00 or 7.00 pm and at 8.00 pm on Friday and Saturday, but the butchers wanted 7.00 pm or 7.30 pm for shops that sold cooked meats. Tobacconists gave a mixed response; some said that, with more leisure time because of shorter hours, sales were up because men smoked more.

The need for money had not abated. This time it was for the Berkshire Voluntary Aid Transport Service. In the papers it proudly stated its achievements and role. Since its formation in March 1915, it had carried upwards of 14,000 sick and wounded soldiers in its twenty ambulances and cars. In addition to the war hospitals in Reading, the service assisted over twenty VAD and other hospitals in various parts of the county. Although all, except three mechanics, were volunteers, the running costs plus repairs and other charges were £25 a week. Donations were urgently needed.

Probably the most unusual request for money was published in a letter to Miss Burnett of 92 London Road. After providing details of the massacre of Nestorian Chaldean Christians in Kurdistan by Turkish troops and Kurds, it requested money to help the refugees. Whether it raised any money or not was never recorded by the papers.

Men and money were the keywords throughout the war. As a result of the German offensive in February, money was needed to assist the French. The number of casualties during the Verdun battles was more than the French could deal with, so an emergency fund was set up to send supplies to France. The Reading War Hospitals Supplies Depot responded generously.

Reading Corporation's trams were very busy and consequently making a good profit but at a cost. At the end of January, J. Silver wrote to complain about overcrowding: 'The public who use the trams seem to have increased out of all proportion to the accommodation provided…and the consequence is nearly all the cars are full to overflowing. You will find people standing on the steps and platform, hanging on to the rail at the back, besides being packed to suffocation inside, which must lead to many illnesses…During wet weather, well, the conditions are simply terrible.' He then went on to respectfully request more up-to-date trams, more seating, covered tops and proper provision for smokers and non-smokers alike, with better ventilation to improve the atmosphere. And that windows that could be opened would be an improvement, with no windows at all in the summer, just curtains. Realising that there was a war on, he politely asked if it could be looked into, but wondered if in the meantime they could just run more trams.

The tramways helped to keep Reading Council going. Accounts give a clear picture of just how well they were doing. To the start of April they had carried 9,953,906 passengers, an increase of 1,072,809 on the previous year. This gave a net profit of £7,485 compared with £4,648 and allowed them to give the council £4,000 for rate relief, helping to reduce Reading's rates by 4d in the pound – it would have been more but for higher wages and war bonuses. Traffic receipts were £40,097 against £35,608. The trams had done more than make a profit; it was proudly pointed out that they had also provided, free of charge, fifty-four cars for the wounded. All this had been achieved because the Corporation had been able to train new motormen and employ women conductors for the first time. The department wrote that great credit was due to these employees for their efficiency after a very short training. These new employees were needed because 118 (59 per cent) of their 1914 staff were now in the forces, a very large number of whom had been fighting for some time. Fortunately, they were pleased to be able to add, so far none had died or been seriously wounded.

This increased employment of women on what had previously been men's work led to more women wanting to be enfranchised. There was no shortage of supporters for the Suffrage Movement in Reading. In early May, under the auspices of the Women's Freedom League, a well-attended meeting was held in the Palmer Hall. The chair was taken by Miss Anna Munro, and the speakers were Miss Nina Boyle and Mrs Despard, three influential suffragists. The league was a suffrage society that wanted votes for women on the same terms as were then or might in the future be granted to men. They argued that the vote was needed then, more so than in times of peace, leisure and prosperity.

Another branch of the Council was also doing well, but unfortunately was not making money. Reading Library and Reading Room had 7,219 borrowers who over the year had borrowed a total of 192,461 volumes at an average daily rate of 709 books. The Central Library issued 151,087 of them. Schools borrowed a further 57,378 books.

While the Council had been doing well, it had been a difficult year for Licensed Victuallers in Reading. At their AGM the problems they had faced were detailed: 'Water charges for trade purposes, assessments of licensed premises, licensed premises held by brewers, restriction of hours of trading, prices of beers and spirits, thefts from licensed houses, serving of wounded soldiers, and serving women on licensed premises before noon.'

The new hours were to be rigidly enforced with custodial sentences of up to six months with hard labour and a fine of £100. Licensed premises, of any description, could sell or supply intoxicating liquor between 12 noon and 2.30 pm and between 6.00 pm and 9.00 pm, except on Sunday when they could open at 12.30 pm. Off-premises sales had the same opening times but closed at 8.00 pm and no one could leave after that time with alcohol. Tick was a thing of the past after 28 February; everything had to be paid for before consumption or taking away. Home consumption of spirits was also strictly controlled, with spirits only available for purchase on a Monday to Friday between 12 noon and 2.30 pm, and only to be taken away during those hours in bottles marked with the name of the premises or club.

These regulations did not sit easily with the publicans. The Vice President of the Reading and District Licensed Victuallers Protection and Benevolent Association, Mr G. Povey, licensee of the Cheddar Cheese in Broad Street, said the order was unnecessary. His reason for disagreeing with the government was: 'Reading was one of the most sober towns in the UK and drunkenness was diminishing each year and there were practically no troops in town.' As the aim of the order was to improve production in munitions factories, his reply was that 'there were no large munitions plants in the vicinity and no labour trouble.' The treating law was easy to get round, and always at the expense of the landlord, and the hours were unfair to visiting farmers in town for market day. He foresaw the closure of many public houses as people stayed home and drank.

Difficult it might have been for the publicans, and contrary to what the Vice President of the Reading and District Licensed Victuallers had said, drunkenness in fact was still a problem, with three cases in one week in Reading. Private William Bellamy of the Rifle Brigade was charged with being drunk in Broad Street; Charles Watts similarly charged but his offence was on the Oxford Road; and Amelia Barry, who had cut her head on a lamp, was taken to hospital on a truck, tried to walk home, and was arrested for being drunk in Redlands Road.

The problem was the same in other towns close by. In Bracknell, Mrs Loder was charged with being drunk. PC Cole had seen her lying on the ground with a basket and quart bottle of beer by her side. She was unable to stand and had to be taken to the Police Station for her own safety. Nearby in Crowthorne, Sergeant Albert Kingsmill and Driver Ernest Brain pleaded guilty to having been drunk and incapable in Pinewood Avenue. Both were brought in unconscious and needed to be attended by a doctor. They had been given a bottle of whisky by a Canadian soldier, Anton Cooper. He pleaded guilty. The offence was serious and could have caused the death of the men. If he had been a civilian, he would have been severely punished, but instead all three were discharged.

Alcohol had been an early target for government regulation. Shorter drinking hours, later opening and earlier closing, increased prices and weaker beer became part of life. The no-treating rule was not a popular regulation and in some areas was not as strictly enforced as others. In the parts of the country subject to Control Orders, areas where war materials were manufactured, 'loaded or unloaded, in transit or dealt with and HM forces are assembled', its enforcement was stringent. In February the Reading, Maidenhead, Windsor and Wokingham districts became subject to the Control Orders. Areas outside the Control Order restrictions were still regulated. The military could and did close public houses to control alcohol consumption. 'In February 1916 it was reported that three public houses in Wantage (then in Berkshire) had been closed...because the landlords had sold drink to wounded soldiers to the detriment of the patients' health.' This is an interesting contrast to the many adverts in the *Chronicle*. The Royal Albert Brewery always indicated that their ale and stout were the preferred beer of the Royal Berkshire Hospital.

Restricted hours would also affect the Post Office. From 1 March, the Head Post Office would close at 8.00 pm, though the public could still send telegrams from the side door in Chain Street up till 10.00 pm. There were no changes to the Sunday hours.

Another Reading and national problem was consumption. In a speech to the first annual meeting of the Reading Tuberculosis

Dispensary Care Association, the mayor spoke of the need to make an extra effort because the country was losing so many men on the battlefield and it was essential to raise a healthy population to replace them. The casualty list was a roll of honour but naming deaths from TB 'would be a roll of dishonour to the country for not taking more adequate steps to prevent the disease'. The worry was made worse because of soldiers, passed for the army, who had relapses on service and who would return along with those who caught it while on active service. 'There had been 50,000 deaths last year, nearly as many as had died in the war.' Reading alone had recorded 861 new cases.

At the end of the year it reported again. In the three months from August to October, there had been forty-four new cases, seventeen of them children. It pointed out that it was the poor who were becoming infected. 'It was found that children sent to the country for fresh air and rest were in many cases inadequately clothed, especially with regard to boots and shoes which were usually of inferior quality.'

Flies were a health issue. In 1915 the local Fly Committee had run a successful campaign against fly-borne diseases using leaflets, visits and free fly-traps. As a result, the war hospitals had been virtually fly free and no cross-infection had been noted. Their work had impressed the military authorities who asked for the same in 1916 because of the threat of typhoid. 'In view of the recent slight epidemic of typhoid fever, the infection of which can so easily be carried by flies…it is to be hoped the good work done by the Fly Committee may be followed up this year by further successful efforts.'

There were problems in the clothing business: with so many in uniform, many shops had surplus menswear. Langston & Sons in Cork Street, known as 'The house of better things at easier prices', cut prices to sell its surplus. 'An offer to the too old, married, and rejected. Men in uniform naturally do not want "Knockabout sport" jackets – you know the style – with the strap back at waist. At this stocktaking we are therefore left with a quantity of these garments, which originally were 16s, 21s, 25s each. Are they of any use to you at 9s a piece?'

By the end of January the report of the 1915 Lord Derby recruitment canvas was available, just a few days after the first men had been called for service. The results make for interesting reading.

Men to be canvassed 8,263
Enlisted or offered 6,208*
Rejected on military grounds 3,000
*Breakdown

	Single	Married
Enlisted for immediate service	462	248
Enlisted for B Reserve	622	1218
Promised for immediate service	0	0
Promised for B Reserve	557	1132
Total promised or enlisted	1642	2597
Rejected by military	979	991
Total	2621	3588
From 1915 unaccounted:		
Foreigners	58	
Dead or over age	90	
Removals traced & details forwarded	198	
Removals untraced	135	
Total	481	

Net unaccounted for – 1494 classed as follows:

	Total Number	
	Single	Married
	3463	4820
Think unfit	223	185
War work, munitions, Marine & railways	59	78
Civil servants, Post Office employees, Police	11	51
Refused permission by employers	26	20
Unwilling:		
a) Subject to conditions	27	103
b) No sufficient reason	213	498
Total	559	935
	16.1%	19.4%

With a deadline of 2 March, the Parliamentary Recruiting Committee asked every 'unmarried man to familiarise himself with the terms of the act and decide to enlist now or attest under the group system before the act comes into force. In order to beat the rush at the last moment, men were urged to enlist or attest now.'

On 14 February, proclamations were posted affecting Derby Scheme and Military Service Act men. It called up all single men to 41 years old, except youths under nineteen. The call-up date was 18 March but so many had been called it was expected to last into April. There were options for deferment and men in reserved occupations could apply to be exempted through the local tribunal. The first of these would be held on 21 February.

Not everyone was happy about conscription. The *Chronicle* noted that 'while in general officials are satisfied with the way men are presenting themselves it was obvious that there was a large number of Military Service Act men (the conscripted) who had an obvious desire to avoid being conscripted.' The tribunal would hear a multitude of reasons why they should not draft a particular man.

With the introduction of conscription, the number of men in industry fell even more. Initially conscription was for unmarried men but in May, the January act was extended to cover all men over eighteen on 15 August 1915 and under forty-one on 2 March 1916. The arrival of War Office Form W326 meant that the recipient was to join the colours and would be treated as a deserter if he did not attend. By September, at Huntley & Palmers, there were 2,765 male employees (many unfit medically because of the work they did, which involved very heavy lifting and high temperatures) instead of over 3,000 at the start of the war. To replace the men, women and boys and girls were employed. The number of women employed had doubled since 1913.

Married men in Reading felt aggrieved by the decisions being reached. In a letter to the *Chronicle*, J.B. Coupland complained of the number of single men with starred trades (exempt) and the many fraudulently given exemption as Conscientious Objectors, putting the onus on married attested men to serve. He suggested that 'even the medical tests were manipulated to give some men release': four council employees were rejected due to poor eyesight but no one else had their eyes tested.

Not every one called was prepared to fight and some would not serve in any way that might be seen as assisting the taking of life. Conscientious objectors of military age who did not report for enlistment were arrested. 'Eleven such were placed for trial at Brock Barracks, Reading and sentenced to 112 days detention.' But it was not only conscientious objectors who did not want to serve. Some, like Harry Bragg, altered their birth certificates so that they seemed over-age; he was fined £20 for the offence.

Local tribunals decided whether a man was exempted or not, but in the latter case individuals were sometimes given leave to appeal to the district tribunal or apply again after a period of exemption. The Reading tribunal of 17 March was devoted to a number of Conscientious Objectors who rejected military service on a wide range of grounds, with some happy to accept non-combatant work in the army or for the state, while others wanted total exemption. Some of the decisions appear random or biased. One GWR employee was rejected while another GWR man, with similar reasons, was given exemption because he had three brothers in the army: one was on war work and the other had just been killed. Mr Deadman, a member of the tribunal panel, thought that his family had contributed a fair quota to military service, and ought to have some consideration. He was exempted, while socialist Edward Johnson, of 37 Hagley Road, who claimed absolute and complete exemption on the grounds that he believed all wars were morally wrong and destroyed national brotherhood, had his claim disallowed. Membership of the No Conscription Fellowship and a belief that only Christ could decide on such an issue as life and death did not gain exemption for Robert Wyatt of 98 Albany Road.

Many of the public saw the Conscientious Objectors as shirkers or cowards, and saw their principles as something to hide behind. It was hard for tribunal panels to differentiate between honest, long-standing Conscientious Objectors and new 'converts'. One case where the Reading Tribunal had no doubts was Henry Taylor, a wholesale grocery and provisions clerk of 159 Elm Park Road. He said he was a recent convert to the Christadelphian sect and claimed absolute exemption. Not convinced there was no link between his impending conscription and his religious beliefs, the panel offered him non-combatant work in the army. When he refused, his appeal was turned down. This meant that, when conscripted, he could be placed in any unit that needed men.

This induced a change in heart and he asked for non-combatant work. Again he was turned down.

Those who refused to acknowledge the tribunals and disregarded their call-up were taken to Brock Barracks and enlisted. Absolutists refused to comply with military commands and faced court martial. Three Reading men and a Reading school master faced a district court martial, presided over by three Majors of the Royal Berks. All had 'whilst on Active Service disobeyed a lawful command given by their superior officer'. James Trustram, 23 The Grove, and Ralph Crammer had refused to take off their own clothes and put on an army uniform. John Coles of 267 Oxford Road had not complied with orders and George Perrin of 6 The Grove had refused to remove his clothes for a medical inspection. All four were found guilty. Crammer, who the paper noted was Jewish, was given eighty-four days imprisonment, the others received ninety-eight.

Some men just chose to ignore the whole process. The first Reading case under the Military Service Act was that of Vernon Ballard of 7 St John's Road. He was charged with being an absentee from the Army Reserve since 18 March when he received his call-up papers. D.C. Henderson went to his house to collect him. Ballard was not prepared to go voluntarily because he did not want to be a soldier but would go if he was fetched. He had tried to get into the ASC and RE but failed and did not want to be in the infantry. As it was the first case, he was fined the minimum of 10s rather than the £25 maximum. His mother paid the fine. He was to be handed over to the military authorities at once. Similarly, Joseph Davis of 2 Union Square did not want to be a soldier. Charged with not presenting himself one day, he absconded and was brought up for the same charge the next day.

When the exemption certificate expired, most joined the army, like it or not. For Arthur Head, of 12 Derby Street, it was the final straw. Attested under the Derby Scheme in group fifteen, he had been exempted at the request of Huntley, Bourne, Stevens, his employer. The 32-year-old reported to the barracks on Friday, 16 June, picked up his uniform, returned home, went back to the barracks the next day and came home late in the afternoon. Then he cut his throat in the scullery. He was found by his parents who went for a doctor. The doctor found him still alive but was bleeding profusely, and he had died by the time the ambulance arrived. He had not threatened to take his life but had

Lord Desborough inspecting C Company of the 1st Berkshire Volunteer Defence Regiment on 21 June.

been troubled by the death of his brother-in-law to whom he was attached; and this had been preying on his mind. A note on the kitchen table read: 'I am sorry, but my head has played me up so. I am not a coward.' At the inquest a verdict of suicide during temporary insanity was recorded.

While many of his flock may well have been trying to stay out of the army, the Reverend T. Guy Rogers, former vicar of St John's, had volunteered for the front and was serving as a minister on the Western Front in 1916. He was awarded the Military Cross 'for conspicuous gallantry and devotion to duty in action. He worked ceaselessly all night under fire, tending and carrying in the wounded. On another occasion, he has done similar fine work under heavy fire.'

What he could not tell anyone at the time was that he had been involved with the execution of a deserter. The Reverend Captain Guy Rogers wrote of his most harrowing ordeal in attending to a condemned soldier.

'31st May 1916. Shall I tell you of the terrible experience I have just gone through (if so it must not go beyond the family circle of yourself). It has just fallen my lot to prepare a deserter for his death, that means breaking the news to him, helping him with his last letters, passing the night with him on the straw in his cell, and trying to prepare his soul for meeting God: the execution and burying him immediately. The shadow was just hanging over me when I wrote the last letter but I tried to keep it out. Monday night I was with him, Tuesday morning at 3.30 he was shot. He lay beside me for hours with his hand in mine. Poor fellow, it was a bad case, but he met his end bravely, and drank in all I could teach him about God, his Father, Jesus his Saviour, and the reality of the forgiveness of sins. I feel a bit shaken by it all, but my nerves, thank God, have not troubled me. Everyone has been so kind who knew of the ordeal. I will tell you more some other time. I want to get off it and away from the thought of it as much as I can.'

At the end of February the weather changed. 'Not since the memorable fall on the last day of April 1908, when hundreds of young birds froze in their nests, had there been so much snow on the afternoon and evening of 25 February.' It continued for the greater part of the next day, Saturday, and made driving conditions very difficult through into Sunday. By Wednesday it had all but disappeared. The Highways Department, with its reduced staff, cleared the snow away as quickly as possible, starting at 4.00 am on Saturday with two large snow ploughs, each drawn by six powerful horses, assisted by thirteen horse-drawn scrapers and rotary brooms, together with about 100 men. By midday the principal thoroughfares were passable. Work continued until late that night. It started again early the next morning with 120 men and 40 horses clearing roads and footways principally in front of places of worship. A letter home from a Caversham man, then farming in Canada, told of similar but much worse conditions. He was experiencing temperatures of 63° below zero, very deep snows – the worst conditions in fifty years.

This was followed by the wettest March in forty-three years. Then, as spring approached, the weather changed. A blizzard caused serious damage in the district. 'Severe gales, accompanied by snow and wind of great violence, swept over the county on Monday and Tuesday (27 & 28 March), and on the latter day was the worst experienced at this time of the year for fully a quarter of a century. In Reading and district rain fell somewhat late on Monday afternoon. Then it turned to snow, but before midnight rain once more descended. On Tuesday, following a dull but fine morning, the blizzard reasserted itself with added violence in the afternoon, and continued for some hours. All the time the wind whistled, slates were hurled into the streets, walls were blown down, mighty trees, chiefly elms, were uprooted, and telegraph and telephone wires were falling practically all around the district. Telegraphic and telephonic communications were entirely cut off from Pangbourne, Basildon, Goring, Hurst, Twyford, Wargrave, Burghfield, Shurlock Row and Sonning.' Large trees lay across the roads; twenty-seven came down in the half-mile between Charvill Lane and Sonning Lane.

Tilehurst was isolated until 29 March as all the roads in and out were blocked by trees. One local, Mr Hilderley, had a narrow escape during the gales. He was cycling along Church Road and as he approached the church an elm landed a foot in front of him. He turned round and another fell, missing him by inches.

Flooding followed the thaw creating a serious agricultural problem. It was impossible to plant the land. Late planting meant a late harvest and consequent food shortages. Reading's sewage went to Manor Farm where the treated waste was used on the 400 acres of arable farmland which had become a boating lake. In places the water was a mile wide. With around 4,000,000 gallons of sewage a day to process and use on the land – treated sewage was used as fertiliser – the floods were an issue on two levels.

Britain relied heavily on imported food. About two-thirds came from abroad at the outbreak of war; in the case of wheat for bread it was 80 per cent. Increased U-boat activity, labour shortages and British military demand meant less food was available, causing prices to rise. By July, food was 55 per cent dearer than at the start of the war and 2.5 per cent higher than in May when potatoes rose 8 per cent. Bacon was 40 per cent more expensive, butter 30 per cent and margarine 18 per cent.

There was severe flooding again. This shows the depth of the water at the sewage farm in Whitley.

At the end of May, meat prices, per stone, at Smithfield were at a record high.

	30th May	Pre-war
English lamb	10s 6d	6s 0d
Scotch (legs)	10s 4d	5s 8d
South American lamb	8s 8d	3s 6d
Home killed English Mutton	9s 4d	5s 0d
Scotch mutton	10s 0d	5s 4d
Pork	7s 4d	4s 0d
Veal	9s to 12s	5s 4d
English Beef (long side)	8s 2d	4s 6d
Scotch beef (long side)	8s 2d	4s 8d
Scotch beef (short side)	8s 8d	5s 2d

Legs and shoulder of English and Scotch mutton from 1s 4d to 1s 5d per pound wholesale.

The Mayor, Leonard Sutton, at the livestock auction to raise money for charity.

There was still plenty of food for those who could afford it.

Prices were rising rapidly and separation allowances failed to match the increases, leaving families with men serving in the forces worse off. Even those in work felt the price rises and, as a result, the National Union of Railwaymen organised a demonstration in Hyde Park against them.

Food crime was taken seriously by the County Bench sitting in Reading. Bread quantity and the quality of both milk and bread gave rise for concern. Both were easily adulterated and it was easy to sell a loaf of slightly lower weight. Messrs Sellwood Bros. of Pangbourne were summoned for selling a loaf of bread otherwise than by weight to a P.C. Charlton. The baker claimed that there was no dishonesty and that he was 'the victim of unfortunate circumstances', in that some loaves shrank more than others and to compensate they always made them bigger. The Chairman of the Bench did not believe it. With the loaf weighing one ounce and four drams less, the baker gained an extra loaf for every twenty-four underweight loaves. The accused was told that it was a serious case as bread was very dear, and poor people needed to be protected and given a fair weight for their money. As the law distinctly said, the bread must be weighed at the time of sale. The business was fined 20s.

Yet another problem, there was now a shortage of allotments. The Board of Agriculture and Fisheries drew the mayor's attention to the necessity of producing as much food as possible from allotments and gardens. In response to this request to boost production, the Small Holdings and Allotments Committee found there was still unsatisfied demand in Caversham and the western parts of the borough. Three areas were proposed: 'the part of Prospect Park upon which house refuse was once deposited and since levelled; land acquired from the trustees of the estate of the late Sir Walter Palmer; the land on Hemdean Road belonging to Councillor Rainbow.' This was still not sufficient and just before Christmas it was suggested that the whole of Palmer Park be dug up for food production.

In the Second World War it was 'Dig for Victory', during the Great War it was rather about thinking about food use and how not to waste it. More and more families cultivated their back gardens and seed sales increased. Luckily for Reading, there was no shortage with Suttons in the town. Cultivation required digging and, during some gardening at home, Mr Deacon of 21 Stone Street found a dead male child. It turned out it had been placed there three weeks previously by his daughter Gertie who was committed for trial at the Berkshire Assizes for attempting to conceal the birth of her male child.

The National Egg Collection for the Wounded meant that there was always a shortage of eggs. Each area of the country vied with one another to provide the most, and at Easter there was a special push to provide even more than normal. The egg collection for Easter of 3,624 eggs put Reading in fifth place out of 2,000 collection centres. The total would have been higher, but many eggs were sent off before the date so hospitals would have a guaranteed supply. During Easter week, 4,038 eggs were collected which would have put Reading in second place. The Egg Collection Committee were pleased with their efforts: since March 1916 they had collected no fewer than 115,196 eggs and delivered 2,700 weekly to Number 1,2,3,4 and 5 War Hospitals as well as Inniscara, St Luke's and Struan House hospitals.

Home-grown food depended on the right weather and sunlight. People also benefit from the sun. The prohibition of lighting during darkness brought daylight saving into prominence. 'Simply through custom, a very large proportion of the people persist in starting work in anything up to half-a-dozen hours after the sun has risen, and leave themselves but an hour or two of daylight (if that) for their leisure hours in the evening. What a great blessing it would be to the multitudes condemned to a sedentary or closed-in life if they could get an extra hour or two per day in the open air with the beneficent influence of the sun!' On 17 May the Daylight Savings Bill was passed.

These were trying times all round. At the AGM of the Reading and District Grocers' Association, an attendee complained that 'it had been a very hard period for the trade. They had experienced difficulties with regard to labour, and in obtaining supplies of goods, whilst the sugar question was a very serious problem. Many traders had to live from hand-to-mouth, as it were, with regard to supplies.'

There was a shortage of money as well and the council did not want to increase salaries. Mr Minckley, the Assistant School Medical Officer, salary £300, was refused an increase of £50 and Mr Simkins, the Head of Wokingham Road School, had his salary increase turned down, even though he was now running the Wilson Street Senior department as well. He was not working longer hours so his salary of £325 was felt to be sufficient.

Inniscara Hospital on Bath Road provided fifty beds. Each ward was named after the benefactor. It opened on 11 March 1916 and closed on 28 March 1919, having treated 913 patients. It was operated by Berks 68 VAD.

In the cause of austerity, at the annual distribution of medals and certificates, Westcott Road Council School gave certificates instead of the usual prizes. Emphasising the change, the school Chairman of the Managers gave the children an address on the need for economy at the present time. The event though was not totally frugal. Nettie Palmer received a silver bar for eight years' perfect attendance.

Again saving money, and time as well, Earley School combined Mayday and Empire Day. The children sang hymns, followed the May Queen's procession and watched her coronation. Miss Joel gave the May Queen a gift.

Councillor F.A. Sargeant replaced Alderman Sutton as mayor during the year.

The theme of the Summer Sales was 'saving money'. 'The magic time of summer sales again approaches, and this year will be warmly welcomed. With prices going up by leaps and bounds, women are glad to seize the opportunity to make the very most of their money.' And, to help, A.H. Bull were offering a number of bargains: 'Muslin frocks at 4s 11d, sports coats at 9s 11d, bright coloured cushions for the river or garden from 1s 4½d, a twenty-one piece tea service for 3s 11½d and a 1000 pairs of lace curtains at a price not to be repeated.'

Not to be outdone, Heelas described their sale as 'a great opportunity for true economy', with white piqué tennis skirts cut full from a small hip yoke at 5s 6d instead of the normal 6s 11d, taffeta coats in tête de negre, green or navy, commencing at 3½ guineas, wide French hand-embroidered Chinese knickers in Nainsook at 2s 9d, artistic Chinese design table cloths on black ground in chintz colourings at 2s 6d, while the 'robe of honour', the overall, was offered at 2s each or three for 5s 11d. Heelas were able to offer these artistic overalls in stripe and spot prints. For those with time on their hands, the needlecraft department offered canvas belts and cushion covers with Allied flag designs tinted in colour for working in wools. 'A fascinating occupation for wounded soldiers with other designs available.'

The Highways Department recommended 2s a week extra for the war for each able-bodied adult carter and labourer but no increase for other workers in the department. As the council needed to exercise rigid economy, £900 extra costs needed a very strong case so further discussion would be needed. Two decisions were made: council wages needed to be dealt with across the board and not by separate departments; no decision could be made at the meeting.

At a special meeting of the Town Council, a wage rise was recommended. Those employed on under 31s a week would be given a 2s a week war rise or such proportion of 2s a week as shall represent the difference between his present rate of wage and regular emoluments and 31s per week. At the same time as expenditure was going up, Councillor Poulton asked for a rate cut of 4d to 6d in the pound. Appealing for a reduction in every way possible, he used the rate cuts in other towns to make his point: Croydon 2d, Wolverhampton 2½d, Ipswich 2d, Northampton 6d, Leicester 5d and York 6½d.

While most council employees were receiving a pay rise, the mayor did the opposite. In line with many MPs and mayors, Leonard Sutton, the Reading Town mayor, gave his salary of £400 to the British Red Cross, after he had taken it in order not to create a precedent for an unpaid mayor.

Corporation wages continued to rise. Shortly after the above increase, the council agreed to a further pay rise for the duration of the war. Motormen and conductors with three or more years' service received 2s 6d a week, for two but under three years' service 1s 6d and over one but under two years 6d. All inspectors received 2s a week. At the same meeting the council agreed to discuss the minimum hourly pay rate set by Sir William Robertson: joiners, bricklayers, carpenters, plumbers: 9¾d, plasterers: 10¼d, painters: 8¼d, workmen employed as hoisters and scaffolders: 7d, and labourers: 6½d.

Reading was running out of affordable housing for the working classes. Although there were insufficient funds to do anything about the problem during the war, plans were drawn up for the immediate post-war period. The Sanitary Committee, having considered the problem, had the borough surveyor begin discussions with the land agent for the purchase of land for housing. The first plot identified was between Silver Street and Southampton Street and would cost £1075. The council also wanted to buy 62 to 68 Southampton Street to add to this in order to provide for a through road and a shop. It was to be purchased within five years of the war ending and, in the meantime, the owners would receive a retaining rent.

With real shortages came a predicted shortage – or was it just a good way to get business before others? Stevens & Co, who have been mentioned before, told readers in their front page advertisement in the *Chronicle* that a coal shortage was predicted due to recruiting and reduced output plus limited and ever-decreasing transport facilities. Naturally, they could help the consumer overcome this problem. They offered to fill a householder's cellar, if the coal was ordered now, at 32s a ton for House Cobbles, 32s 6d for Bright Cobbles and 30s for Scotch Nuts. In order to be certain of supplies, the order had to be made in May. For those unable to afford coal, they also offered wood blocks at 14s and peat at 12s 6d a load.

Later the company played the threatened shortage for all it was worth: 'The state requirement of 10,000 miners as tunnellers for the front, in addition to the very large number already recruited in to the

Army, bids fair to virtually paralyse the coal industry from the domestic point of view. Coal supplies under these circumstances will not only be short, but probably extremely scarce next winter. Those who are sufficiently alert to provide for the coming dearth by filling their cellars while they CAN get coal, will profit by their wisdom and avoid a hardship which will press heavily on the many.'

Boating on the river was a part of Reading's life that not even a World War could stop. May saw the opening of the river season as usual with 'Messrs Maynard & Sons launch *Britannia* running trips to Goring and Henley on specified days at popular prices. To go to Henley or Goring for 1s return in wartime is one of the cheapest forms of travel to be obtained.' Teas and minerals were provided on board. As well as the steam boat trips from the boathouse at Caversham Bridge, other types of pleasure boats were also available and there were punts for hire.

One problem that should have been sorted out by 1916 was the registration of enemy aliens. A court case in May showed this was not the case. It was discovered that Alfred Bruckner, a German citizen born at Ultona, had failed to register as an enemy alien. Superficially, it seemed simple, but the case was adjourned for advice when it was discovered that the accused was a sergeant in the 3rd/1st Berkshire Yeomanry. Investigations found that he was a German businessman involved in dubious deals and bankrupt. His defence was that he only wanted to serve the country. He was sentenced to six months' hard labour.

Fortunately, with so many men away, there was no increase in crime. It did, however, continue and was recorded weekly from the local courts. In the middle of the year, just prior to the Somme offensive, Reading magistrates dealt with the theft of a parcel, child neglect, bike theft, showing too much light, cycling on the footpath, having a fruit barrow on Broad Street and using a home for immoral purposes. The heaviest sentence was reserved for a brother and sister. Florence Bryant, aged twelve, and her younger brother were both sentenced to time in an Industrial School for petty pilfering at school.

Like most cities, towns and villages across the country, Reading was affected by the losses of the Somme battles. However, many deaths occurred in the run-up to the 'Big Push' and not just in the attack area. As the offensive started, the parents of Second Lieutenant A.F.J.

Monsieur Jean Sosman, the Sanger of Flanders, was appealing against an order of the Reading Justices to destroy his faithful mare, when this photo was taken. He and his son had fled from the Germans on the horse after they had destroyed the circus and seized and shot the animals.

The Woodclyffe Hall in Wargrave became a war hospital. The soldier, centre right, is Fred Armitage who was wounded on 1 July serving in 34 Division.

Burnham received official notification and, as was normal, a letter from an officer in the battalion with details about the death, sometimes with more detail than was needed. Albert's parents, James and Emily Caroline, who lived at 'Ladysmith,' Western Elms Avenue, Reading, received such a letter from his captain: 'You will have heard by now of the gallant death of your son on the night of 28-29th, but I must write you just a line to let you know how much we all felt his death. Ever since he joined me in B Company he has been loved by officers and men alike; he was always so cheerful and full of life that he was just the man we want out here. His Platoon – number 5 – I know miss him very much, as he was always thinking of them, and it was while cheering them in the midst of a heavy bombardment that he met his death. He was just lighting a cigarette on the fire step when a shell hit the top of the parapet and then took the top of his head off; he was, of course, killed at once. He was buried yesterday in a military cemetery near here (Kemmel Château) and I have just visited his grave...He was such a good friend to me that I find it impossible to express my feelings at his loss, but I trust you will realise how much you are sympathised with by us all out here.'

Pte. H. COXHEAD, Royal Berks Regt., 52, Newport Road, Reading.— Wounded.

Pioneer S. WHICHELOW, Royal Engineers, 52, Newport Road, Reading. Wounded.

Stepbrothers wounded around the same time during the opening stages of the Somme offensive.

As in 1915, the papers showed the importance of one young man's death over all others, this time in sentiment rather than column space. In April, the *Chronicle* told its readers the flower of England's manhood was giving its all for the Empire's existence. Few would have disagreed with this or how two deaths, in the same issue, could be reported so differently. Class was (and perhaps is still) so important. 'There have been many heavy sacrifices during this war, but one of the most poignant is that in which the one and only child, the heir to a large estate, the hope of his parents and of the tenants and employees connected with the property, falls a victim in the undiscriminatory ravages of war. It is for this reason that the thoughts of all go out in special sympathy with Sir Charles and Lady Henry, of Parkwood, Wargrave, in the death of their only son, Lieutenant Cyril Charles Henry.' He was killed by machine gun fire at Loos on 26 September.

The above is in direct contrast to the death of another only son, Lance-Corporal Percy Upton. His death was reported without the flowery language or messages of sympathy. The difference: he was a working boy from Catford who had joined the Royal Berks in June 1915 while he was working in Newbury. Up to the time of his enlistment, the 27 year old was a music hall artiste – Perce Jerome of Jerome and Jerome, patter comedians. The chaplain wrote to his parents: 'I know it will be a great shock to you; nevertheless it will be some comfort to know he gave his life for others. I am sure that God has accepted his sacrifice...in the cause of right.'

Not all the volunteers were young and single. Many older, married men with children had also joined to do their bit. Among the Reading casualties at the start of the Battle of the Somme was Corporal Vincent Saunders. Married, with a family and a steady job at Huntley & Palmers, he was 37 years old when he was killed in action on 3 July. He was one of only six fatalities when 5 Battalion attacked at Orvillers and just one of a thousand employees on war service.

Captain William E. Blandy who was wounded when charging enemy positions under heavy machine gun fire on 14 August while serving with the 1st/4th Battalion in France. He had been at the front since March 1915.

*Another local casualty.
Nineteen-year-old
Private William Charles
Vockins, son of William
and Emily of Kennett
Cottages, Burghfield,
died of a head wound in
Southall hospital on 4
October. He was a
Kitchener volunteer and
had served in France for
over fifteen months.*

At least Corporal Saunders' family could be contacted because he had given his family's home address. This was not always the case when sons had emigrated and lost contact. A typical case was that of Private D.H. Haynes, 16953, 7 Battalion Canadian Army. He had given his next of kin as J. Haynes of Chatham Street but, on the soldier's death, his next of kin could not be traced. The borough police were anxious to make contact as there was money owed to Private Haynes' family.

Along with the casualty list and the death obituary, many families reported a son's death in the traditional way: a private death notice. Many were brief because of the cost, others stated the facts and some provided a personal poem or a stock-poem, like the one for the 21-year-old signaller, Private Fred Painter, youngest son of Henry and Mary, of 6 Dover Street:

POPULARITY !

About 18,000 (Eighteen Thousand) people, nearly a quarter of the whole population of Reading, visited this Store on the first day of our July Sale, and general astonishment was heard on all sides at the wonderful Bargains displayed.

FIRST DAY.

Thursday, July 20th,

At 9.30 a.m.

FRESH RELAYS

OF

REMNANTS

EVERY

DAY.

Just twenty days after the start of the biggest battle of the war, McIlroy's were pleased to announce the success of their sale.

'Somewhere in France there is a grave
Where sleeps a son amid the brave.
No father or mother saw him die
To kiss his face or wish him goodbye.
He heard the call, he gave his all
Away in that foreign land.'
From his sorrowing mother and father.

Typical obituaries and wounded notices for the Somme period included: 'a pathetic circumstance with the death of Second Lieutenant Norman Clayton, Royal Berkshire Regiment, on July 23rd, is that it followed very closely that of his younger brother (Public School Corps), who was killed on July 20th. Second Lieutenant Norman Clayton's death is greatly mourned in his battalion. Moreover, a fine scholastic career – has won an MA at 21 – has been cut short.' 'News has been received by a corporal of the Berkshires that Private Ernest John Cook, whose parents reside at 103, Wykeham Road...has been killed...mortally wounded and...he died within three minutes, being shot through the body...leaves a widow and three children.'

In the same edition, a Bradfield casualty notice encapsulated the experience for many Reading and Berkshire families: 'Great sympathy is felt with the widow of Private E. Green of the Royal Berks. She is left with four small children.'

Even the usually joyful birth notices could be a poignant reminder of the town's sacrifices. 'On 2 August, at 14 Lower Vine Buildings, the wife of Private Albert Day, Royal Berks (DOW on 20 July), a daughter' – a daughter who would never know her father.

While most of the casualty lists were for soldiers, after a major naval engagement, the paper carried both comment and casualty details. After Jutland, which was fully covered in the morning daily papers, the *Chronicle* recorded sombrely that 'thousands of our gallant seamen have found a watery grave in the Jutland fight, whilst the nation has to mourn the loss of Lord Kitchener...we believe...Jutland was just as much a turning point in the naval war as the Battle of the Marne was in the land, and as Verdun is today.'

Regarding Berkshire's contribution to this great victory, it noted that the county had always provided large numbers of men for the Royal Navy. 'In spite of the large losses, their parents should be filled with pride at the great deeds their sons performed, at their determination and courage in facing such odds, and their splendid heroism in death.' To emphasise the sacrifice, the *Chronicle* published two full pages of photographs and a page of biographies of the local men who had died at Jutland. Typical of these are the following: Seaman Allan Woods was lost when HMS *Indefatigable* was sunk. He had been in the navy for ten years and lived at 48 Granby Gardens. Able-Seaman Paxford, of Leopold Road, was twenty-two when he was lost in the sinking of HMS *Tipperary*. His father was in the army. Stoker Charlie Wake was lost when HMS *Invincible* sank. He was the youngest son of Mr and Mrs Wake of 88 Erleigh Road. He had been in the navy for four years.

The careers of the wounded were often reported, sometimes in great detail and with much pride. 'CQMS W.J. Smith, of 659 Oxford Road, serving with the Royal Berks, has been wounded – fractured forearm and dislocated elbow. He is the third son of Mr and Mrs Smith of 51 Pell Street, and was educated at the Reading Blue Coat School. He served in the South African War with the Imperial Yeomanry, and received the QSA with five clasps. He enlisted as a private soon after the commencement of the war, and quickly rose to the rank of sergeant. After passing the School of Musketry as a qualified instructor, he was appointed Sergeant-instructor of Musketry to the battalion. He was promoted to CQMS a few weeks before proceeding to France. Before enlisting he was a motorman in the service of Reading Corporation Tramways. He has two brothers serving…'. Most were much shorter: 'Private W. Edginton, Royal Berkshire Regiment, of Woodley is wounded and in hospital.'

When HMS Hampshire *sank, among those lost were a number of men from Reading. Gunner Percy Baker was one of them.*

Twenty Reading men serving together on HMS Empress of India*.*

The dichotomy between the fighting front and the home front is clearly shown by the holiday traffic carried by the Great Western Railway, much of it through Reading. 'In the summer of 1916, when the flower of the nation's manhood was dying on the Somme, seasonal holiday traffic reached such proportions that the *Cornish Riviera* was leaving Paddington daily in three sections carrying an average of 1,400 passengers.' The volume of excursion traffic in July and August was so great that clerks had to be drafted in as emergency porters.

Huntley & Palmers were generally seen as a benevolent employer but nevertheless did encounter some problems. In late June, the girls in one room of the biscuit factory ceased work because of an internal dispute. Many of them assembled outside the factory and one of the forewomen was escorted home. Within three days the dispute was settled, the women returned to work the next day and the forewoman was reassigned. On the Sunday there was a demonstration requesting a 5s increase a week for Huntley & Palmer employees.

The dispute generated a number of letters to the paper about behaviour. An ex-soldier recorded disorderly scenes in the vicinity of the factory and wondered why Special Constables were not used to protect those who wanted to work. He pointed out that a man of sixty-two had his hat knocked off and was half throttled because he wished to do his bit. He noted the irony of the situation: 'It was a trifle humorous to see a gang of girls singing... "Keep the home fires burning" and at the same time handing out blows to those who wished to do what they were singing.'

In reply 'A Factory Girl who knows' pointed out that: 'it was impossible to keep the "home fires burning" on the wages she was receiving at the price that things are now. And for doing our bit, we did ours when we worked three nights a week overtime and could barely manage on it. Perhaps the "Ex-soldier" has more income than we. Therefore, he understands little of what it means to feed and clothe a wife and five children on 21s a week or a girl to keep herself respectable on 7s 6d a week, not forgetting the 6d war bonus. Those who did not come in to do their bit will take their extra money with smiling faces, and also with guilty consciences, knowing that they little deserve it, not having helped in the least to get it. The old man of 62 was not pushed but fell over himself in trying to push through those who were doing their bit. In every opposition you always find spies.'

This was not to be the end of this particular matter and in 1917 another strike engendered further bitter feeling.

As a result of the action, wages were increased. Men, twenty-one and over received a 5s increase, men and lads sixteen but under twenty-one 3s, lads under sixteen 2s, girls or women over eighteen 3s, girls under eighteen 2s. At the same time all war bonuses were abolished.

This was followed by a similar dispute at Serpell's with employees asking for 5s a week and a similar increase in proportion for all other employees and with a fixed rate for piece work. With union involvement, most of what was asked for was conceded by the management and work quickly recommenced.

Each week the papers carried a casualty list that got longer as the fighting became more severe. Usually somewhere there was a story about bravery, luck or just plain fortitude. Corporal F. Bowler, a Reading-based GWR shunter, fell into the latter category. He was a reservist, recalled at the start of the war. During the Mons retreat on 10 September on the Marne, he rescued Lt. A. Knight, carrying him 400 yards across open shell-swept country under heavy rifle fire, for which he was mentioned in Sir John French's dispatches. He was wounded on the Aisne and twice at Ypres and Zonnebeke and invalided home. In March 1915 he was shot through the arm at Festubert and wounded again at the end of March 1916. He survived the war.

For the loved ones of those on the casualty list, it was a time of anxiety. When her son was gassed in October, Mrs Ellen Paul wrote to his unit for information: 'Dear Sir, Can you please send me news of my son, Sapper R. Paul, 137959. R.E. 24 General Hospital, Etaples, France, who was suffering from Gas Poisoning. I had a letter 10 days ago from him saying he felt a little better & was in a convalescent camp, and he could not send his address as he was going to be moved the next day again but as I have not heard since I am feeling very anxious. Trusting you will be able to let me have news of him soon. Yrs Respectfully, Ellen Paul.'

Bravery was seen at other places besides the front. In October, RFC Second Air Mechanic S.G. Stevens of 56 Blenheim Road exhibited bravery for the sixth time in his life. He was recommended to the Royal Humane Society for saving the lives of three young men who had capsized a punt near Caversham Bridge. When he saw them he took off his cap and tunic, dived in and got all three to land. In 1910 he had saved a boy near Caversham lock, before which he had rescued a baby in a perambulator and also a child who at Caversham lock, had fallen down the steps into deep water. After attending Redlands, Kendrick and University College, Reading, he had worked as an Assistant Master in Midsomer Norton where he extinguished a fire at the Wesleyan Chapel. Then in 1915 he had stopped a runaway horse.

There was a considerable RFC presence in and around Reading by the end of the war. During the year 'a recently built jam factory in Coley,…was taken over for use as a technical training school for the Royal Flying Corps. Headquarters was at Coley Park House.' Its purpose was to train fitters and riggers in groups of 125 over a five-week course. These then went on to active squadrons. Flying training was based on a field near the Kennet. 'By 1917 hundreds of members of the Corps were billeted in south Reading homes during the winter months, but were under canvas in Coley Park during the summer.' When the RFC and RNAS merged, the technical training school was moved to Halton.

In October the School of Instruction formed at University College in December 1915 had merged with the School in Oxford to become No. 1 School of Military Aeronautics with headquarters at Yeomanry House. The main classrooms were in Wantage Hall where aerial reconnaissance and radio were taught, with requisitioned accommodation across the town.

The family 'competition' in providing men for the country's service continued in 1916. April saw two families, the Minchins and the Richens, proudly providing eight male relatives each for the colours.

Men of the RFC parading before going to church.

The 237 Field Company, RE, raised and trained in Reading, leaving Wantage Hall for the front, in January.

Sons of Mrs. HAMBLIN, widow, 72, Chatham Street, Reading.

Across the country, Mrs Hamblin must have been at the forefront of families contributing the most sons to the armed forces. There is no record of any of them dying during the war. Mrs Hamblin was a very lucky mother.

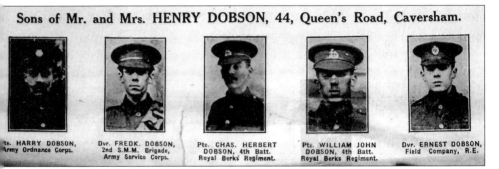

Sons of Mr. and Mrs. HENRY DOBSON, 44, Queen's Road, Caversham.

Another lucky Reading family. None of Mr and Mrs Dobson's sons are listed by the CWGC.

Only officer losses were named in the first issue after the opening of the Somme offensive. The paper gave the names of the ten officers killed, the two who died of wounds and the eleven wounded. Whilst providing a whole page of officer and other ranks biographies, it simply told readers that losses amongst the rank and file had been considerable.

It also provided personal stories about the battle and individuals' deaths. One upbeat reminiscence was provided by Private Charles Thatcher, a 28-year-old GWR employee of Bembridge Place, who was recovering from a bayonet wound in the thigh: 'I must think myself very lucky that I got over with what I did. It was horrible out there – to hear all the guns firing and to see some of your mates blown up in the air… you would have laughed if you could have seen old Fritz stove (sic) when we got amongst them with our bayonets. They did run, and shouted "Mercy, Kamerads".'

The following week featured the biggest 'Roll of Honour' of the war to date, which clearly indicated the scale of losses in middle class families: Second Lieutenants G.M. Courage and C. Goodford, both only children, and Second Lieutenant G. Dandridge, an only son. The parents of many decided on an endowment named after their son. A typical gesture was the provision of a hospital bed or equipment. The

Not many men survived having twenty-three wounds. Private E. Weeks, Royal Berkshire Regiment, of 180 King's Road, did and survived the war.

Field Marshal Lord French at Reading Station prior to inspecting 1 Battalion Berkshire Volunteers on 8 October. On Lord French's right is Lieutenant Colonel Benyon, Lord Lieutenant of Berkshire.

Prisoners in Germany pose with their armed guards showing that in some camps there were good relations between enemies. The sailor in the centre is Arthur J. Brock, of Tilehurst.

plaque above a bed in Benyon Ward was dedicated to their son and only child 'one of the cheeriest and the best,' by Major Dr and Mrs Ritson, who endowed the bed in memory of their son, Captain John Andrew Ritson, BA Cantab, a Trinity scholar. He was killed 'in action whilst gallantly leading his men' of the 7th South Lancashires, on 23 July, at the Battle of the Somme.

As soldiers writing home or to the papers were careful not to give their whereabouts, the letters, like Private Thatcher's above, could be quite detailed enough to give the civilian some understanding of what their soldier friends experienced. Some provided a personalised view as did Private Pritchard, of 73 Katesgrove Lane, serving with the 1st/4th Royal Berks: 'It was real murder, but thank God we came out alright. Bert Day and Len Gibbons were wounded. Poor little Day was blown about fifteen feet in the air and got both legs broken; Gibbons got one leg broken and his other foot smashed. It was a miracle I and Tom did not get hit. We had just finished our dinner and were sitting on the fire-step, when a shell came over and up went the lot. Three were killed outright and several others wounded. It was perfect hell, they were shelling us all day…you should have seen the chaps reading their Bibles, and waiting to see who was going to be next.'

Although the Royal Berks were experiencing severe casualties, there was no let up on the demand for cigarettes. Once again the

Military Medals for Four Berkshire Men.

Cpl. Bandsman SIDNEY C. SMITH, Royal Berks Regt., 51, Pell Street, Reading.

Lce.-Corpl. C. COLLINS, Royal Berks Regt., 36, Coley Terrace, Reading.

Spr. SLADE, R.E., of the "Dreadnought," Thames Side, Reading, while in a V.A.D. Hospital at Kettering learned of his award.

Pte. T. D. RUSSELL, of Sonning, who was educated at the Kendrick School, Reading, and at University College.

Casualties and awards filled many column inches.

Another flag day. This one is for the Red Cross.

Tobacco Fund was short of money and, as the Somme battle was raging, it proudly boasted how much it had done so far in 1916. Between 24 December and 10 July it had sent out 'nearly three millions of cigarettes, three-and-a-half tons of tobacco, 180,000 cigars, 2,000 pipes and 25,000 local papers' to the 7,000 men at the front. The lack of funds meant that no more papers would be sent out. Even with

A badge sold to raise money for the Church Army Hut Fund.

prizes, hand-made by men of 4 Battalion, such as a Royal Berks cap badge carved out of chalk blocks taken from a building on the Ypres front, they could only raise half the £800 needed.

Reading obviously thought more of the YMCA than its local Tobacco Fund. In one day, the citizens gave £1,250 to the YMCA Hut flag day. The money was to provide huts that soldiers could use when on leave.

The military lives of former Reading F.C. players were popular. Lance Corporal W.G. Bailey described a typical experience in the trenches. He felt that they had been lucky, even though they had taken over new trenches and spent a longer time there than usual. There were always casualties; the number was comparative. 'We had two footballers wounded the last night – Summers of Grimsby, and Gray of Dundee; they were in my section. I must say it was lucky I saw the rifle grenade coming, or it might have wounded more. I was only four yards from them, and a piece cut my lip and nose, and I did not notice it till one of the boys said to me "Your face is covered with blood." I thought it was blood from Gray, as I took him in my dug-out to dress him.' Bailey was commissioned later in the war and was awarded the MC and bar before being demobilised.

T.R. Rogers of Tilehurst was commissioned after winning the DCM.

Around the same time, Alan Foster, the Reading centre-forward, returned home on leave. Looking fit and well, he told readers that the Reading players were in good health, though Summers, the Reading goalie, had been wounded. As in Reading, there had been snow and

Harold Roberts at school. Son of Thomas and Mary of Caversham Lodge, he is buried in Karasouli Military Cemetery in Greece.

rain and the conditions in the trenches were most disagreeable. On a positive note, they were as well fed as they were in England.

While football suffered from a lack of available talent, resulting in Reading F.C. suffering financial problems, one sport that kept going throughout was whippet racing. There was no shortage of entrants or people to watch. It had its own track opposite the Pulsometer Works on the Oxford Road. Their annual Good Friday handicap started at 2.00 pm prompt; any dog 'not on their marks at the proper time' was disqualified. The club promised good entries and a capital afternoon's sport. Admission was 6d. Ladies and soldiers were half-price.

The wounded were treated well in Reading, with visiting concert parties, trips on the Thames, outings to local beauty spots or just tea at a large house. Villages held whist drives for them and invited them to their fetes. One Reading businessman, Sol Joel, was a benefactor to the Earley Defence Force and to the wounded. He provided land for the former and entertained the latter in his wooded park, Maiden Erlegh. Using the resources at his command, and assisted by the Earley Entertainment Committee, he held a large garden party at the end of May for sixty-five wounded men from Reading's war hospitals. With tea and refreshments provided by the hosts, the committee organised football, cricket, ships' quoits, bowling, donkey riding and boating on the lake. 'A hat-trimming competition created the utmost amusement.'

Most of the war stories concerned the activities of the various Berkshire units but there were frequent notes and letters from those serving at sea, as many Reading men were. A brief letter from

Christmas Holidays.

A. H. BULL, Ltd.,

Beg to announce to the Residents of Reading and District, their Patrons and Friends that they have decided to close their Business from Saturday EVENING, DEC. 23rd UNTIL FRIDAY MORNING DEC. 29th & they respectfully hope that customers will lend their kind consideration and support to this effort to grant the staff a well deserved rest.

An unusual and financially risky request. Whether the employees were paid for this holiday is not clear.

YMCA picnic for the wounded who were transported to Peppard Common by motorcycle sidecar and cyclecars. The motorcade gathered in Market Place before setting off.

one is representative of most received and, like others, involved being lucky when sunk. Harvey Williams, of Seaford Road in Wokingham, serving as a marine gunner, was in the engagement between the commerce raider *Greif* and HMS *Alcantara*. Both vessels were lost. Of the 300 men on the *Greif*, only five officers and 115 men were picked up and made PoWs. British losses were five officers and sixty-nine men. Williams was in the water eighty minutes before rescue. He was sent home for a fortnight to recover from the shock.

There was still a shortage of men for the army, but it was now realised that men over the military age could nevertheless be employed

Summer sports day at Bear Wood, a hospital for Canadian soldiers.

*On the right is D.R. Baldwin of 52 Shaftesbury Avenue, Reading. Aged seventeen
and a half when the photo was taken he had already been in the navy over a year.*

by the army. Suddenly men over the age of forty-one and under forty-
seven could enlist. The army wanted 1,000 men, accustomed to work
on railway construction and other constructional and building work, to
enlist in 30 Railway Labour Battalion. They would be paid 3s a day to
serve in France with a RE Railway Company.

This further reduced the number of men available for civilian work
that required strong, physically able men. As a result of conscription,

1st BATT. BERKS VOLUNTEER REGIMENT.

A and B COMPANIES, Platoons 1 to 8.

Orders for week ending November 13th, 1916.

Sunday.—Parade King Edward Statue, 8.40, for Didcot. Train leaves 9. The band will attend.

Monday.—Shooting: No. 8 Platoon, Alfred St. range, 6.30 to 8.30; Caversham range, 6.30 to 8.30. Recruits' class, Armoury, 7.30.

Tuesday.—Shooting: No. 4 Platoon, Alfred St. range, 6.30 to 8.30. Class for recruits and members wanting instruction, Armoury, 7.30. Band practice, St. Giles' Hall, 8.0.

Wednesday.—Parade Armoury, 3. Swearing in of recruits, Armoury, 7.30 to 7.45. Enrolment forms may be obtained from Mr. Rydill, The Arcade. Shooting: Caversham range, 6.30 to 8.30.

Thursday.—Shooting: No. 5 platoon, Alfred St. range, 6.30 to 8.30. Recruits' class, Armoury, 7.30.

Friday.—Shooting: No. 1 Platoon, Alfred St. rang, 6.30 to 8.30; No. 2 Platoon, Alfred St. range, 7.30 to 8.30. Special instruction, Armoury, 7.15.

Saturday.—Parade, Armoury, 3.15.

The Alfred Street Range is open to all members of 1, 2, 4, 5 and 8 Platoons daily.

CALCOT PLATOON.

Sunday.—Platoon drill with newly-formed Englefield Platoon at Englefield at 2.30. Conveyances at Calcot parade ground 2 o'clock.

William Alfred Kirke, 69 Wolseley Street, was invalided out of the army during 1916. Somehow he managed to rejoin his regiment, the KOSB, and returned to the front. He died on 31 July 1917 and is commemorated on the Menin Gate.

The week's orders for Companies A and B of the 1st Battalion Berkshire Volunteer Regiment.

the Berkshire Lunatic Asylum was unable to recruit male staff. All its male nurses had enlisted under the Derby scheme. As the number of inmates was only down by six over the year because patients from Buckinghamshire and Middlesex were now admitted, they were facing a severe staff shortage.

To bury the dead required the skills of a coffin-maker and, by late 1916, men with these were scarce. Mr C.H. Lovegrove had to fight to keep his only remaining coffin-maker of military age, A. Hopes, who was thirty-five and had been passed as fit only for sedentary work. Mr Lovegrove told the tribunal that he held the contracts for burying all the soldiers who died in Reading, and contracts also with the Guardians and other public bodies. He had lost six men to the military and could

There were no concerns about the raising of the pension age in 1916. The Stevens brothers were employed by the Highways Department of the Reading Corporation. When the photo was taken their joint age was 216 and they had served as corporation workmen for 130 years. On the left is the youngest brother, Frank, aged sixty-nine with forty-five years' service. In the centre, Tom had worked for the corporation for forty-three years and was aged seventy-one. Joseph, on the right, was the eldest, at seventy-six but had the shortest service, a mere forty-two years.

get no replacements. The tribunal gave Hopes a month to settle his affairs, but told him he could apply again for exemption.

Whilst small in number compared to the many military deaths, the newspaper stories of individual deaths were equally sad, as many were lives cut short. A headless female body on a railway track and a farmer found hanging in his barn showed the pressures that some could no longer live with. Then there was the short story of 12-year-old Eric Pirie's discovery. Playing on Chapel Hill in Caversham, Eric found a black bag protruding from a rabbit burrow. Sensibly he fetched his uncle, Special Constable Walter Gale, to inspect the parcel. It was found to contain the 'greatly decomposed remains of a child, wrapped up in a piece of cloth and some brown paper and tied with string.' The medical report could not state the cause of death because the fully developed child had been dead about a month. There was a police investigation but no follow up story.

Grief was given as the potential cause of death of one local, Mary Warrick, aged sixty-four, of 45 King's Road, a widow, who died from heart failure as a result of shock. Generally in excellent health, she went to bed feeling unwell on Thursday evening and stayed in bed all Friday, complaining of a headache. She was found dead that evening. During the week she had been informed that her son was wounded and had received a letter calling up her deceased husband. She had cried seeing this envelope, thinking her other son had been killed. In September 1915 she had lost a son, another was wounded and another was in France. The post-mortem showed an enlarged heart with flabby muscles. The cause of death was acute dilation of the heart – heart failure. The doctor suggested, with reason, that grief and worry about her sons might well have caused her death.

The production of food was essential for the war effort, but this became difficult as so many men were claimed by the army. At a farmers' conference in October, they stated that they had reached 'the absolute limit, but still the reckless demanding of the land of labour went on'. They could bring in the harvest with women, roadmen and pensioners, but they could spare no more skilled men who attended cattle, sheep and the carting. Any further loss of labour would affect crop production. Eventually the authorities realised that certain jobs needed skilled labour and gave guidelines to the tribunals as to the number of men who were required to be left on a farm. To provide further help on the land, 626 boys under fourteen were allowed to leave school for farm work during the year,

Children were also helping the war effort in other ways. The Reading Education Committee Report for the year ending 31 March 1916 showed that schools and Manual Instruction Centres had been busily engaged in making articles for the military hospitals. This included '2,596 splints, 101 bed and leg rests, 261 bed tables, cradles and trays, 51 foot rests, 18 bandage winders, 432 crutch heads and handles, 84 pairs of socks, 8 pairs of mittens, 1.015 shirts and vests, 89 handkerchiefs as well as coats, scarves, stockings, jackets, mufflers, helmets, pillow slips, slippers and bandages.'

The seriousness of the situation at the front was made clear to workers in Reading by a letter from the Minister of Munitions to the mayor, referring to the postponement of the August Bank Holidays. This was due to the urgent need to maintain an undiminished output of munitions. The mayor told workers that it was necessary that all holidays, not merely those of workmen directly engaged on munitions, be postponed and that a holiday atmosphere should be avoided. He felt he could rely on the cooperation of the employers and work people of Reading in this matter in order to help the Allies carry through the battle in France to a successful issue.

A rather different letter in the same issue drew people's attention to another, perhaps less vital issue. It was about 'the disgraceful things going on, especially on Sunday evenings, in that part of the arcade leading to the public lavatories for both sexes. There is continuous horseplay and indecent remarks and behaviour going on for the best part of the evening, and part of the time it is really not fit for a respectable woman to walk up there. Could not some Special Constable keep an eye on this part instead of the outskirts of the town, where there is not so much supervision required?' The writer signed off with 'hoping to see a pleasant change in this district'. There was no reply or further letter from this writer. Perhaps things changed or they changed to a different route?

The second anniversary of the declaration of the war was celebrated by a special united service at Trinity Congregational Church. In the evening at a mass meeting in the large Town Hall, the mayor said 'they met with very different feelings from what on August, 4, 1914, they had expected to have. Instead of being able to look back on the great

The Victory Loan Barometer in Broad Street outside the Information Bureau.

battle of 1914, to end in peace before Christmas – as some of them had expected – a continuous battle had raged through the whole of 1915 and the greater part of 1916.' He concluded that 'everyone was more determined than ever that the great cause they had taken in hand should be carried through to a successful issue' at which the audience cheered. Naturally the meeting closed with the National Anthem.

Another shortage became apparent when the government issued

details of the wool purchase scheme, good news to Berkshire farmers but not to householders. All of the 1916 clip of wool became the property of the War Office, leaving none spare for civilian clothing. This was to ensure that the military had sufficient and also that it could be exported to other Allied countries for war purposes.

Two police raids made the news in September. The first was carried out by Inspector Walters, accompanied by Sergeant Purdy and Constable Henderson. They entered the premises of the No Conscription Fellowship under instructions from the military authorities and took possession of various undisclosed documents. This aroused little interest compared with the raid on Reading Football ground. The 'Hunt up' had become a common way for the police and military to catch men who had escaped the vigilance of the military authorities. At the match, everyone of military age or thereabouts had to pass inspection and those who were not known or failed to produce the correct documents were detained. Many had simply left their papers at home and were resentful at the inconvenience, but with the borough police and military police supported by large numbers of soldiers from the King's Liverpool and the Devonshire Regiment, there was no resistance. The ground was cleared in thirty minutes and, after papers were inspected, forty-two were marched to the Town Hall for further enquiries. Some of the detained had come from London, Portsmouth and Basingstoke to see the match. All claimed to be in munitions work or were in the process of obtaining War Service badges. It was subsequently ascertained that none of the forty-two were liable under the Military Service Act to be in the army. The next week the military admitted to the ineffectiveness of such raids that labelled a man a coward or slacker because he forgot his papers.

A month later the police were in the news once more when ex-Police Inspector Frank Staite of the Reading Police Force was indicted, at the Berkshire Assizes, on eleven counts with embezzling sums of money, the property of His Majesty, amounting in all to £107, between 15 September, 1914 and 30 November, 1915. He was further charged with mutilating a locomotive handbook, the property of the mayor, Aldermen and Burgesses of Reading, and also with unlawfully, wilfully, and with intent to defraud, omitting certain material particulars from the Police Department cash book, viz., the eleven sums of money. He pleaded not guilty. After lengthy cross-examinations and a summing

With the ever present threat of an air raid many people took out extra insurance. As Reading was not a priority target this company felt able to provide a reduced rate.

up by the judge, 'without leaving the box, the jury, after consulting for three minutes, returned a verdict of guilty.' The judge told the defendant that he had a position of trust, and, although of good character, he had to be punished. He was sentenced to nine months with hard labour.

Staite was given leave to appeal a week later. At the Court of Criminal Appeal his appeal was dismissed and he went to prison.

On the night of 1 October residents saw a once-in-a-life-time fire. The Zeppelin L31 had been caught in the searchlights and shot down over north London. The glow was easily distinguishable from Reading. Among those who saw 'a brilliant flame' falling to earth was Police Sergeant Martin. Many other residents and police officers also reported it.

In November, Reading was able to boast that one of its own was a Zeppelin destroyer. Lieutenant Cadbury, a Quaker, and son of George Cadbury of Bournville, together with two other pilots, was responsible for the destruction of LZ61. Cadbury's connection was that he had gone to school at Leighton Park. Two other ex-Leighton Park pupils were also highlighted: Captain Alan Lloyd, DSO (The CWGC only holds a record for a Lieutenant Alan Lloyd, MC) and Private Raymond Ashby, DCM who was commissioned for successfully taking twenty-four unwounded Germans prisoner while he himself was wounded in four places.

Besides the many reports of brave deeds and medals won at the front there was also bravery on the Home Front. Four months after her courageous action, Louise Wakeman, thirteen, was presented with a silver watch and £5 cheque from the Carnegie Hero Fund. This was in recognition of her bravery in June, when she jumped in to the Thames, fully dressed, at a spot where it was sixteen foot deep, and rescued 6-year-old Sidney Turner from drowning. After bringing the boy to the bank she carried him home on her back. She had been taught life-saving.

RFC Second Air Mechanic S.G. Stevens of 56 Blenheim Road was a brave man.

Civic pride extended to the care of the wounded. An appeal was addressed to the women of Britain and the Empire to raise £50,000 to build the Star and Garter Home for Disabled Soldiers and Sailors. Reading's contribution was yet another flag day. The target was £2,000 for a 'Reading Room' in memory of the Royal Berkshire Regiment.

After coming through its financial problem, Reading F.C. now faced its other difficulty. It was getting more and more difficult to get together a regular team. They decided to withdraw from the London league, and were replaced by Portsmouth. They then had to decide if occasional fixtures could be played.

In the financially stringent times of late 1916, it was essential for shops to attract customers. W.J. Garrett, clothier, hatter and hosier for men, youths and boys in West Street, came up with a gift that would appeal to its clientele. In the paper he 'informed his numerous friends and clients that he had ready for presentation, a striking portrait of the ever popular and famous Field-Marshal, the Rt. Hon. Earl Kitchener of Khartoum'. He was pleased to present one to all customers who spent 5s or more, if the customer requested it.

In the general gloom came a glimmer of light for the employees of Huntley and Palmers. The board

One of the more expensive badges produced to raise money. This is multi-coloured and has a gold surround. Later in the war flags had a tag and no pin to save valuable steel.

The husband and wife team of Mr and Mrs Medland of 774 Oxford Road, supplied horseshoes to the army. Mr Medland shaped the shoes and his wife and assistant flattened them at the rate of 116 a week.

had responded to an application by the Reading branch of the National Union of Gasworkers and General Labourers for a bonus. From 17 November there would be a weekly raise of 3s for men, 2s for women and 1s 6d for boys and girls.

Although the business was doing very well, the biscuit factory was not without its problems. The recently-introduced war flour, mixed with all sorts of other cereals to economise on wheat imports, was not of sufficient quality for biscuits. This twenty-four per cent adulteration contained too much gluten to make biscuits. Without white flour there would be no export sales, and this would result in a loss of £5,000,000 in revenue.

While the factory was having problems with flour, everybody was having difficulty in obtaining firewood which was now becoming expensive. Fortunately someone came up with a replacement: 'Take any old newspaper, roll each page into a rather tight roll, give it a few twists and then tie it into a knot. Three of these placed on a little loose paper in a grate (treated just as if you were using wood), with coal on top, will make a splendid fire in a few minutes.'

Even though there had been a bumper harvest of potatoes, prices were rising. This was blamed on two factors: London prices were affecting the rest of the country and farmers holding supplies back to maximise their incomes.

There was another shortage at the front that Reading women were asked to alleviate. Taking the initiative were the volunteers at the War Supplies Depot who did a two-week knit for the troops. Locals were urged to copy their lead and buy the wool at 4s 6d a pound and knit mufflers, mittens and helmets to send to the BEF. These would be added to the list of goods supplied over the past year: 84,047 articles in textiles such as bandages, bed-jackets, mosquito nets and 20,182 of wood and metal such as bed-rests, wire arm cradles, crutches. All these were made by volunteers.

University College, Reading, now found a new role. It was recognised by the Ministry of Munitions as a training centre. It offered training to men and women of superior education and those who already had a trade in machine tools. Successful completion guaranteed employment. Within a short time after the courses started, over 3,000 18-pounder shells had been turned out.

The tribunals and their outcomes were thoroughly reported, presumably to make it clear to the townspeople why some men were not being drafted. With government exemption, there went a level of security from brickbats for the exempted and their families. Some applications were obviously self-motivated, some were for sound family reasons. Others were so obvious that it beggars belief that the tribunal had to waste its time on them, while in some cases it was unclear whether the applicants were telling the truth or not.

It is interesting to speculate why a military man, Major Price, knowing the army was desperate for men who had been passed as fit for general service, would apply to keep his chauffeur, W.F. Tune, who was twenty-eight and fit to fight overseas. This was a second application because he could find no replacement. When told a woman could do the job, he offered to pay a commission to anyone who could find a suitable female. Mr Tune was given a final exemption until 1 January. The tribunal sensibly granted conditional exemption to 29-year-old council employee F. Page, because he was a widower with four children, but why T.J. Alderson was called up is a mystery. He had resigned from the borough police due to ill-health but was only granted conditional exemption even though he was infirm and suffered from extreme deafness. At the County Appeals Tribunal, he was given the choice of military service or munitions work. However, the single, B1 category (suitable for garrison service abroad), 29-year-old dairyman, F. Pym, who was still selling milk at a lower price than other dairymen, was exempted until 1 February and given leave to apply again.

Two cases that were not straightforward came before the tribunal panel in early December. What would be the reader's decision on them, given that they had to be examined and graded before they were called up? A.E. King from Lower Caversham, a 25-year-old motor driver for Heelas, said he was the sole supporter of his widowed mother. He had been discharged from the regular forces (soldiers received official discharge papers) on the ground of consumption (a notifiable disease) and had been medically examined three times since his discharge yet he was still being called-up. The panel adjourned the case for two weeks so that papers and information could be obtained.

On the same day, the son of a deceased Caversham councillor, Thomas Stacey, an 18-year-old single man, employed as a junior clerk at GWR Paddington, claimed he was not fit to be in the army. He had been passed by army doctors as fit for general service but he produced a note from his own doctor (perhaps a friend of his late father?) that claimed he suffered from asthma and had a functionally deranged heart (increased, or excited action, defective, or enfeebled action, and irregular action). He was given three months before he was to be called up again and was allowed to appeal.

With Christmas looming, it was natural for stores to start advertising their Christmas goods but in a more subdued way than the previous two Christmases. And to make sure purchases were completed on time, the Early Closing Association informed the public that most stores would be closed for three days, 25, 26 and 27 December.

The next price rise was for a Christmas commodity. Holly was very scarce and was fetching up to four times its usual price. However, there were still plenty of Christmas trees around at up to twenty-five feet in height.

Like the holly, money was in short supply and with so many wounded soldiers in Reading the Care and Comforts Committee

Inspection of 1st Battalion Berkshire Volunteer Regiment.

appealed for funds. With 1,800 wounded to provide for, £100 a week was needed. This would allow them to provide fruit and cakes, outings and entertainments, books, tobacco and hospitality to relatives. They had enough for Christmas but nothing after that.

German PoWs from Holyport made the news just before Christmas with another breakout. Twenty-seven-year-old Leutnant Cruentek and twenty-four-year-old Leutnant Thelen of the Flying Corps escaped from the detention centre and made their way towards London. They were recaptured in Old Windsor wearing brown suits. On questioning, one claimed to be Swiss, the other from Kent. Noticing their accents, the Police Constable asked them to accompany him to the station which they did without resistance. It had been a well-planned escape. Admitting their identities, Thelen cursed his luck: 'This is the third time I have got away, I must be unlucky.' Each possessed 5s and between them had a bar of chocolate and a London map. Their exit had been undetected because they had been bound round with waste paper, and to get air had a pithless stick of elder wood to suck and blankets to rest their heads on. They were wheeled out of the camp, past the guard, in barrows, and were placed in the waste paper store outside the grounds. When they were alone, they simply broke the lock and left.

Soccer played an important role as outdoor entertainment over Christmas with a number of games. At home in Elm Park, Reading played the ASC on Christmas Day, the 1st Footballers Battalion on

Alas no more but at Christmas 1916 E. Jackson's was a busy, thriving store.

Boxing Day and the 1st Reserve Regiment of Cavalry the next day. Visiting players included Private Billy Henry of Manchester City, Hammond, a South African international, Slavin and Boynton from Hull City, and Quinn (Grimsby and Southampton). Playing for Reading were A.M. Stevenson of Everton, J.W. Skinner from London, Sergeant Price of Wolves, A. Hinton from Southampton, A.M. Butterworth, Millwall, A. Scott of Hearts and A. Ford from Arsenal.

Reading's financial stringency was reflected by the work done by the Post Office over the Christmas period. Christmas 1916 was the lightest on record, so light that the Christmas Day delivery went out on time. However, it was still 'a time of stress and strain', even though the 200 men serving in the armed forces had been replaced by

permanent temporary staff. To deal with the increased volume o.
required an extra sixty-three female and thirty-five male staff .
deliveries and ninety females and six males indoors sorting. A
temporary parcels office had to be opened at the Queen's Head to
relieve pressure and make sure the 3,000 army allowances were paid
each week to Reading residents.

This was reflected by the traffic volume of the railways. A
commentator noted that 'there was a patriotic response to the
government's appeal to the nation to do as little travelling as possible
at Christmas, and railway officials reported on the quietest Christmases
for some time.' Neither the passenger nor the goods trains were over-
taxed, and the traffic was lighter than that of an ordinary weekend.

The third Christmas of the war was more sombre than its
predecessors. A journalist recorded his thoughts: 'while there had been
no lack of amusement available, either in football or in the indoor
amusements, all well patronised…Christmas (had) been essentially one
for the fireside, and the dark nights and slippery pavements…
contributed to a stay-at-home holiday.' To another observer, Christmas
1916 would be remembered as 'Foggy Christmas': 'Seldom have the
streets of Reading been enveloped for so many hours at a time.'

Even so, efforts were made to make sure that the poor children of
Coley and the soldiers in the war hospitals enjoyed the festive season.
Increased poverty in the Coley area was caused by the rise in prices
and, to help families, the Education Committee decided to continue its
traditional Christmas Day breakfast for around 300 children. The meal
was served in St Saviour's Hall and consisted of ham sandwiches, cake,
bread and butter and tea. They 'fell to with a will' after grace and a
welcome from Father Thurston. On leaving they each received an
orange, a Christmas card and a bun.

The inmates of the gaol were Christians and many were not enemy
aliens. As it was Christmas and a time of goodwill, one would have
thought they might get a more Christmas based meal than they did.
Their menu was bread, potatoes, peas or beans, hot mutton and
pudding. However, those with money could buy roast pork and
stuffing. Everyone was given wine with their meal and those who
wanted could purchase beer, even interned Germans.

At the RBH, a Christmas dinner of turkey and plum pudding was
served at midday. 'After dinner the chief attractions were the bran tubs

provided by the Care and Comforts Committee.' During the remainder of the day, impromptu concerts were held on the wards where 'considerable talent was found amongst the patients.' Everything was done at the various war hospitals to make it a bright and cheerful day for the wounded. The consensus was that everyone 'had a most enjoyable time'. Wards were decorated and large quantities of traditional Christmas fare was provided. There was a Whist Drive and music and games were played. At St Anne's hospital in Caversham, Father Christmas arrived during the meal and handed out gifts.

A sobering thought for those working in the war hospitals was the sheer number of patients. During the year 118 convoys of wounded soldiers had arrived and discharged 508 officers and 6,700 men.

The worry of many families for their loved ones put an edge on the cheer of Christmas, all the time waiting for the dreaded telegram. A Reading architect and his wife, William and Louisa Howell of Heronden, Cintra Avenue, received just such a telegram over the

A Christmas card sent from the front by a soldier in the 1st/4th Battalion.

Every year there was a collection to send Christmas puddings to the troops. This is the card used for the 1916 collection.

Christmas period. Their son, Second Lieutenant N. Howell of the KSLI, aged nineteen, who had been in the army for a year, had been home on leave on 6 December and returned to France on 16 December. A week after his return to France he was shot in the head by a sniper. Another son Second Lieutenant R.B. Howell was missing and believed killed.

In an end of year report, the borough engineer acknowledged that the war had affected his ability to construct new works due to rising costs, manpower shortages and the cost of labour. There were some improvements: Bridge Street had been widened, Morgan Road had been paved and provided with sewerage, and the footpath from Caversham lock to Clappers footbridge had been improved. Twenty-three-and-a-half miles of road had been tar-sprayed. This sort of work was unlikely to continue because the army were asking men with road-making skills to enlist for such work in France and the council had agreed to loan the army what machinery it could spare.

Which department was the most successful in 1916? Once again it

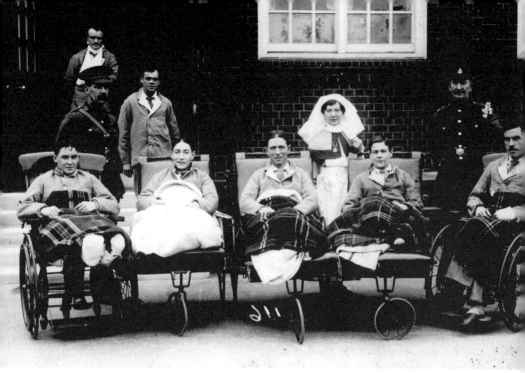

Amputees at the Reading War Hospital. The two soldiers on the left both look very young.

The staff, Berkshire Corps of Women Volunteers, and inspecting officers of the Inniscara War Hospital on Bath Road. It was opened as a Red Cross convalescent hospital that provided massage treatment. In the front centre is Vice-Admiral Fleet; on his right is the matron, Mrs Lambert.

Wounded leaving for a constitutional along the Oxford Road.

was the tramways. It was their most successful year with receipts £4,404 higher than 1915. After paying the allowances of employees, it had made a net profit of £6,232 and was able to give £4,000 for rate relief. The department was pleased with its efforts. It had provided fifty-four free cars for wounded soldiers, was employing sixty-three women as clerks, conductors and inspectors, and with seventy per cent of its staff serving with the colours, it was providing a better service than before the war. It was also lucky: only three of the 140 men serving had been killed. One, Sergeant Wilson, a conductor had been awarded the Military Medal. Extra income from the government came

A Furber hand ambulance carriage purchased with money from yet another collection for 8 Battalion Royal Berkshire Regiment.

Manufacturing shell cases in the engineering works of Huntley & Palmers – every shell was 'like a piece of jewellery'.

to the tramways in the form of munitions contracts for the manufacture of high explosive shells – the 1917 contract was treble the 1916 contract – and from the RFC using half the tram sheds and the employees' social club rooms.

As well as taking over buildings, the RFC also requisitioned land, some for practical use, some for leisure. 'During the early war years the ground at Kensington Road was made available for wounded soldiers' recreational activities but in 1916 it was requisitioned by the RFC as their recreation ground.' Here throughout the war, they played many cricket matches against local teams.

Once again the libraries had proved their worth. Excluding school loans, 194,116 volumes had been borrowed at a daily average rate of 716 books and there were now 7,072 borrowers. An important difference between 1916 and pre-war was the male-female ratio: it was now almost 100 per cent female. To accommodate the number of wounded in the town, it was decided to close the West Branch library to the public for the duration.

Not wishing to be outdone, the waterworks was able to contribute £2,000 for rate relief, because, despite the rising cost of coal, it had been able to offset costs. And with a reduced staff it had managed to maintain water purity and provide sufficient water during periods of absolute drought, 13 July to 11 August. On one day, 3 August, it was able to provide 4,268,000 gallons, a million in excess of an average day's consumption.

It had been a year of anxiety and difficulty for the town's schools. The merger of Reading School and Kendrick Boys' had been approved. Kendrick Girls' was full, but with no money available, expansion was not planned until after the war. Six elementary schools were still in use as hospitals and the displaced children were educated in a double-shift system at the other schools. And worse was the absence of fathers due to military service. It was felt that this had 'bred a disregard for discipline which...needed a strong hand on the part of the teaching staff to correct'. Paternal absence had resulted in the growth of juvenile crime.

Finishing the year on a positive, Public Health had, on the whole, been good. The high incidence of cerebro-spinal meningitis in 1915 was much diminished with only twenty cases being reported. While the first half of the year had seen large numbers of measles cases they had all but disappeared in the second half. Scarlet fever and diphtheria numbers were half the average, but there was an unusual outbreak of enteric fever in widely separated parts of the borough during the first quarter. This was blamed on the many military cases brought to the war hospitals from abroad. The low birth and death rate were the same as 1915.

It had been a long and hard year – but there was something to look forward to in the New Year: the Heelas sale which started at 9.00 am on Monday 1 January. Gazing into the crystal ball, Heelas advised potential purchasers that there would be more shortages to come. Although January was typically 'a month of economies', rising prices meant it was better to buy now and not wait. The Heelas advert told the public 'in spite of the many great difficulties you are able to secure unusual values at this sale'. It advised them to take advantage of the offers 'to the fullest possible extent, as all the markets' were showing

Girl Guides furnished a guard of honour at the wedding at St Peter's, Earley, of Lieutenant Montagu Hartcup, ASC, of Bungay, Suffolk and Miss Winifred Weldon, daughter of Colonel F. Weldon of Earley.

unprecedented rises. As a result, woollen, cotton and linen goods would 'not only be very dear' but also 'extremely difficult to procure'. And with the government commandeering the leather supply, Heelas recommended an early viewing of their huge stock of high grade boots and shoes before they were all sold.

The Reading weekly papers made no comment about the future although they did encapsulate the past and its achievements. The year

1917 was a New Year with no predictions. One thing they knew for certain was that train travel would become more difficult. The number of trains to be run was reduced and journey times would increase, often quite considerably. There would be no restaurant cars and the famous *Cornish Riviera Express* would not run, it would be replaced by an ordinary service. Worse than the reduced service – some lines would not run at all.

Not all serving men were young. The headstone of H.J. Stevens, aged 50, in Early Churchyard. HMS Vernon *was a torpedo school based in Portsmouth.*

Chronology

Chronology of the war at home and abroad
This shows some of the major events that were happening at home and
on the battlefields.

1914
August
1 British ships detained in German ports.
2 German troops invade Luxembourg.
3 The king of the Belgians appeals to King George V for diplomatic
intervention to safeguard Belgian integrity. Germany declares war
on France.
4 Germany declares war on Belgium. British mobilisation orders
issued; 1st Battalion Royal Berkshire Regiment is mobilised at
5.30 pm and 1st /4th Battalion at 7.20 pm. British ultimatum to
Germany ends with a state of war at 11 pm.
5 Britain mobilises for war. Lord Kitchener becomes Secretary of
State for War.
6 Appeal for 100,000 men to join the army.
7 BEF begins to land in France. The Prince of Wales inaugurates the
National Relief Fund.
8 Defence of the Realm Act (DORA) passed.
10 Aliens Restriction (No. 2) Order stopped enemy aliens engaging
in any banking business without written permission from the Home
Secretary.
11 Press Bureau constituted. First Battalion Royal Berks ready to
proceed to the front after inspection by the king and queen.
12 Great Britain declares war on Austria-Hungary. First train carrying
the 1st Battalion leaves Farnborough at 10.27 am.
13 1st Battalion arrives at camp near Rouen.

17 Enrolment of Special Constables begins.
19 1st Reserve Battalion formed – became 5th (Service) Battalion.
20 Queen's Work for Women Fund launched. 2nd Battalion Royal
    Berkshire Regiment leaves India.
23 1st Royal Berks in trenches near Mons.
24 Retreat from Mons begins. 7th (Service) Battalion formed.
28 Appeal for a further 100,000 men for the army.

September
5   First Battalion Royal Berks fighting on the Marne.
8   Speech by Lloyd George on the need for economy.
12 6th Battalion formed at Shorecliffe.
13 1st Battalion Royal Berks fighting on the Aisne.
18 Trading with Enemy Act passed imposing severe penalties by way
    of fine and imprisonment upon any person trading with the enemy.
28 Lord Fisher appointed as First Sea Lord after resignation of Prince
    Louis of Battenburg.
?? 8th Battalion formed at Brock Barracks.

October
10 2nd Battalion arrives in Liverpool.
16 First Canadian troops arrive in England.
23 1st Royal Berks fighting at Ypres.
24 Importation of sugar prohibited.
29 Turkey enters the war on the German side. National Union of
    Women Workers' Police Patrols officially set up by the Home
    Office.

November
4   2nd Battalion Lands in France.
5   Great Britain declares war on Turkey and annexes Cyprus.
9   Prime Minister gives a speech at the London Guildhall setting out
    the war aims of the Allies: 'We shall never sheathe the sword'.
11 Parliament opens.
14 2nd Battalion in trenches at Fauquissart.
17 Lloyd George's first war budget.
29 King leaves England on a visit to the army in France.

December

6   Pope tries to bring about a Christmas truce.
16   Scarborough, Whitby and Hartlepool bombarded by the German navy – 137 killed and 592 injured.
21   Seaplane air raid on Dover – no casualties.
24   Aeroplane raid on Dover – no casualties.
25   Seaplane raid on Dover – no casualties.

1915

January

19   Zeppelin air raids on Yarmouth and King's Lynn – 4 killed and 16 injured.

February

4   Germany declares waters round the United Kingdom a war region as from 18 February.
21   Aeroplane raid on Colchester and Essex – no casualties.

March

5   Issue of 3% Exchequer bonds announced.
5   Bill introduced to give government power over munitions works.
6   Thirty-four Trade Unions agree to expedite munitions output.
10   2nd Battalion engaged at Neuve Chapelle.
16   Customs (War Powers) Act allows Customs and Excise officers to confiscate and condemn any goods suspected of being of enemy origin.
30   Home Secretary appoints a committee of enquiry into the recruiting of men from the retail trades. 1st/4th battalion lands in France.

April

5   King George prohibits use of alcoholic drinks in any of the royal households.
7   Appeal by the churches for restraint in the use of alcohol.
13   Munitions Committee meets under the chairmanship of Lloyd George.
14   Zeppelin raid on Tyneside – 2 injured.
15   Zeppelin raid on Essex and Suffolk – no casualties.

16   Aeroplane raid on Faversham, Sittingbourne and area – no casualties.
20   Prime Minister at Newcastle denies that British operations are hampered by a lack of munitions.
22   Passenger traffic between England and Holland suspended.
29   Zeppelin raid on Suffolk – no casualties.
      Lloyd George announces the government scheme with regard to alcoholic drinks – a drink tax.

May
4   Budget estimated expenditure £1,6632,654,000 introduced; estimated revenue £270,332,000. Drink tax abandoned.
7   Zeppelin raid on Southend – 1 killed and 2 injured.
      Lusitania torpedoed off south west coast of Ireland. 1,198 men, women and children drowned including 124 US citizens.
10   Anti-German demonstrations in London and Liverpool as a result of the sinking of the *Lusitania*.
12   Anti-German riots.
14   Internment of enemy aliens begins.
16   Zeppelin raid on Ramsgate – 2 killed and 1 injured.
19   Age limit for recruits fixed at 40.
25   Coalition Ministry formed.
26   Zeppelin raid on Southend – 3 killed and 3 wounded.
30   First air raid on London when Zeppelins raid East London – 7 killed and 35 wounded.
31   5th Battalion lands in France.

June
4   Zeppelin raid on Kent, Essex and the East Riding – 8 injured.
6   Zeppelin raid on Hull, Grimsby and the East Riding – 24 killed and 40 injured. One Zeppelin destroyed by Lt. R. Warneford, RN.
15   Zeppelin raid on Northumberland and Durham – 18 killed and 72 injured. Daily cost of the war now £2,666,000.
16   Lloyd George takes the oath as Minister of Munitions.
19   Ignatius Trebitsch Lincoln, ex-MP for Darlington committed for trial on charges of spying.
24   Prime Minister announces forthcoming bill on the registration and organisation of national resources.

25 Coalition government formed under Prime Minister Asquith.
29 National Registration Bill introduced by Mr Walter Long. This required the registration of all people between the ages of 15 and 65 resident in England, Wales, Scotland, Scilly Isles and (with reservations) in Ireland.
31 Welsh miners' dispute settled.

July
2   Ministry of Munitions formed.
4   Aeroplane raid on East Suffolk – no casualties.
12 South Wales miners' conference rejects government proposals.
13 £570 million (besides £15 million through the Post Office) subscribed to War Loan. Strikes made an offence.
14 National Registration Bill passes the House of Lords.
15 Welsh miners' strike begins.
    National Registration Act becomes law.
17 Women's right-to-serve procession starts at the Victoria Embankment, London, organised by Christabel and Emmeline Pankhurst and the Women's Social and Political Union.
20 Welsh miners' strike settled.
26 6th Battalion lands in France.

August
2   6th Battalion in the trenches.
8   National Relief Fund stands at £5,431,671 in one year.
9   8th Battalion lands in France.
9   Zeppelin raid on Goole, East Riding, Suffolk and Dover – 17 killed and 21 injured. One raider destroyed at Dunkirk when returning to base.
    Zeppelin raid on Essex and East Sussex – 6 killed and 24 injured.
15 National Registration of all males and females aged between 15 and 25 years.
16 Cumberland coast bombarded from sea – no casualties.
16 Zeppelin raid on Kent, Essex and London – 10 killed and 48 injured. 8th Battalion go into the trenches.
31 South Wales coalfield dispute finally ended after considerable government concessions.

September

7 Zeppelin raid on East Suffolk and London – 18 killed and 38 injured.
   Unrest among railway workers in South Wales.
8 Zeppelin raid on London, Norfolk and the North Riding – 26 killed and 94 injured.
9 Lloyd George stirs up Labour at TUC Congress: 'With you victory is assured, without you our cause is lost…This country is not doing its best.'
11 Zeppelin raid on Essex – no casualties.
12 Zeppelin raid on Essex and East Suffolk – no casualties.
13 Aeroplane raid on Margate – 2 killed and 6 wounded.
   Zeppelin raid on East Suffolk – no casualties.
16 Taff Vale railway dispute ended.
17 Debate in House of Commons on National Service.
20 7th Battalion arrives in France.
21 Budget introduces new taxes; 50 per cent on excess profits and on certain imports on grounds of foreign exchange and luxuries. Raised taxes – by 40 per cent on income tax; postal charges; imports of certain comestibles, tobacco, motor-spirit, patent medicines. Exemption from income tax limited to £130; scale of abatements on larger incomes reduced.
24 Liquor control regulations applied to the areas of Greater London.
25 8th Battalion attacks Hulluch.
30 Labour meeting resolves that the voluntary system with special recruiting campaign is sufficient and that there is no need for conscription.

October

7 Labour leaders appeal for volunteers for the army.
11 Lord Derby produces recruiting scheme; forty-six call up groups with married men being the last to be called-up. Treating prohibited.
12 Edith Cavell executed at Brussels.
13 Zeppelin raid on Norfolk, Suffolk, the Home Counties and London – 71 killed and 128 injured. 8th Battalion fighting at Loos.
15 State of war between Britain and Bulgaria from 10.00 pm.
23 King George appeals for more men.

28   King George thrown by his horse while inspecting troops in France. 'L2' circular setting out women's wages for munitions workers.

November
1   King George returns to England after his accident.
6   Suspension of *The Globe* for publishing misleading statements about Lord Kitchener.
8   Drastic criticism in the House of Lords of the government's measures, especially the press censorship.
11   Lord Derby warns unmarried men of compulsion if they fail to enlist voluntarily before 30 November.
26   Mr Stanton, Independent Labour candidate stands as a protest against pacifist and anti-recruiting policy of late Keir Hardie, and wins the seat by 4,206 votes.

December
11   Rush of recruits to volunteer during the last two days under the age group system. 7th Battalion leaves France.
12   Lord Derby's recruiting campaign closed.
16   New 5% Exchequer Bonds issued at par.
20   Derby groups of single men called up. 7th Battalion leaves Alexandria for Salonika.
24   7th Battalion arrives in Salonika.
25   The king sends Christmas message to his troops.
28   Cabinet decides for compulsion – single men before married men.

1916
January
4   Lord Derby's report on recruiting published; of the five million men of military age only half had offered themselves for enlistment.
5   Military Service Bill introduced which prioritised the order of those who would be called up.
22   Aeroplane raid on Dover – 1 killed and 6 wounded.
23   Air raid on Kent – no damage.
24   Military Service Bill passed by Commons.
25   Protest against closing of London Museums. Labour conference decides to allow its members to remain in the cabinet.

31 Six Zeppelins raid West Suffolk and Midland Counties – 70 killed and 113 injured. War Savings Committee inaugurated.

February

9   Air raid on Margate and Broadstairs – 3 injured. Military Service Act comes into operation. Extension of restrictions on lighting and on sale of sugar.
14 Remaining classes of single men called up.
15 Speeches on the war by Mr Asquith and Lord Kitchener.
20 Aeroplane raid on Kent and East Suffolk – 1 killed and 1 injured.
21 Lord Robert Cecil appointed Minister of Blockade. Peace debate in Commons.
26 Government recognises National Volunteer Force for Home Defence.
    Proclamation creates a blacklist of forbidden companies and people with which trade is expressly forbidden.

March

1   Aeroplane raid on Broadstairs and Margate – 1 killed.
2   Lord Derby speaks in the Lords on recruiting – system of exemptions criticised, especially in the case of agriculturalists; women must take the place of men.
5   Zeppelin raid on Hull, East Riding, Lincolnshire, Leicestershire, Kent and Rutland– 18 killed and 52 injured.
6   Women's National Land Service Corps inaugurated.
14 Army estimates in Parliament allow for pensions for those discharged owing to illness contracted on service with 4/5ths full pension if aggravated by service.
15 Lord Derby's pledge to married men with regard to military service.
16 South Wales coal dispute decided; miners must join recognised unions in order to maintain output.
17 Food prices risen 48 per cent.
18 Royal Defence Corps formed.
19 Four seaplanes raid Dover, Ramsgate, Margate and Deal. Little material damage but 14 civilians killed and 26 wounded. One raider brought down at sea by Flight Commander Bone, RNAS.
20 Central Tribunal for Great Britain set up.

31 Army Council takes over hay and straw. Zeppelin raid on
    Lincolnshire, Essex and Suffolk – 48 killed and 64 injured. One
    intruder destroyed.

April

1   Zeppelin raid on Durham County and North Yorkshire – killed 22
    and injured 130. Zeppelin L15 captured. King George presents
    £100,000 for war purposes.
2   Powder explosion in Kent causes 172 casualties. Resumption of
    work advised by Clyde strike committee.
    Zeppelin raid on East Suffolk, Northumberland, London and
    Scotland – 13 killed and 24 injured.
3   Zeppelin raid on Norfolk – no casualties.
4   Budget introduced with new taxes on amusements, matches and
    mineral waters.
    Income tax varying up to 5/- in the pound. 50 to 60 per cent
    increase in taxes on sugar, cocoa, coffee, motorcars and excess
    profits. Zeppelin raid on East coast – 1 killed and 9 injured.
5   List of certified trades under Military Service Act revised.
    Zeppelin raid on Yorkshire and County Durham – 1 killed and 9
    injured.
6   First married groups called up.
12 Clyde strikers tried for sedition.
17 Committee appointed to investigate recruiting. Committee held
    that there was no case for extension of Military Service Act to all
    men of military age, but suggested extension of the act to include
    those reaching the age of 18; the retention of time-expired regulars;
    further combing-out of single men and perseverance with existing
    methods of recruiting.
18 Lord Milner advocates universal military service in the House of
    Lords.
20 New Volunteer regulations issued. Manpower proposals to be
    submitted to secret session of both houses. Sir Roger Casement
    lands in Ireland and is arrested.
    Disguised German warship *Aud* sunk while trying to land arms on
    the Irish coast.
24 Outbreak of the Irish Rebellion.
21 Zeppelin raid on Lincolnshire, Cambridgeshire, Norfolk and

Suffolk – 1 killed and 1 injured. Aeroplane raid on Dover – no casualties.

Rebellion in Ireland – Sinn Feiners seize Dublin Post Office; serious fighting in the streets of Dublin.

Yarmouth and Lowestoft bombarded from sea by German cruiser squadron – 4 killed and 19 injured.

22 Martial law in Dublin.

German battle cruiser squadron raids Lowestoft – engaged and dispersed by local naval forces.

Great Yarmouth bombarded – 4 killed and 19 wounded.

Zeppelin raid on East Suffolk, Kent, Essex and London – 1 person injured.

23 Zeppelin raid on Kent – no damage caused.

24 Martial law across Ireland.

New Military Service Bill abandoned.

27 Dublin Post Office burned by Irish nationalists.

30 Dublin rebels surrender.

May

1 Zeppelin raid on East coast of England and Scotland.

End of Irish uprising – leaders surrender. Total casualties for the uprising: military and police, killed 124; wounded and missing 397; civilians killed 180 and 614 wounded.

2 Zeppelin raid on Yorkshire, Northumberland and Scotland with 9 killed and 30 injured. Zeppelin L20 sank off Norway.

3 Aeroplane raid on Deal – 4 injured. Three Irish leaders shot. Military Service bill extending compulsion to married men is introduced.

9 Appeal of Irish nationalists to support the constitutional movement.

Duma (Russian parliament) members received by King George.

10 Commission appointed to enquire into the causes of the Irish rebellion.

11 Debate in Parliament on Irish administration. Mr Asquith announced the execution of twelve Irish rebels and that he would visit Ireland in the near future. In total 73 sentenced to penal servitude and six to imprisonment for life.

12 Mr Asquith visits Dublin.

15 Sir Roger Casement charged with high treason.
16 Military Service Bill extending compulsion to married men passes the Commons.
17 Daylight Saving Bill passed.
18 Royal Commission on Irish rebellion opens.
19 Air raid on Kent and Dover – 1 killed and 2 injured. One raider destroyed over the Belgian coast.
21 Daylight Saving Bill comes into operation.
22 Daily cost of the war recorded as £4,820,000.
23 Munitions workers' patriotic procession.
25 Military Service Act becomes law.
    Lloyd George undertakes settlement of the Irish question.
    According to the king's message to his people 5,031,000 have voluntarily enrolled since the start of the war.
27 2nd/4th battalion lands in France.

June
5   HMS *Hampshire* mined off Scottish coast when proceeding to Russia: Lord Kitchener and his staff drowned – 75 bodies washed ashore, 12 survivors recovered.
8   Compulsion replaces voluntary enlistment in Great Britain.
15 Daylight Savings Act comes into operation.
25 Trial of Sir Roger Casement begins.
29 Sir Roger Casement found guilty of high treason and sentenced to death.

July
1   On the first day of the Somme battle, 2nd Battalion attacked at Ovillers and 5th Battalion at Montauban.
2   5th Battalion in action at Ovillers la Boiselle on the Somme.
3   Report of the Royal Commission on the causes of the Irish Rebellion issued. 5th battalion attacks near Ovillers on the Somme.
4   Ignatius Trebitsch-Lincoln, ex-MP, sentenced to three years in prison for forgery.
6   Lloyd George becomes Secretary of State for War, with Lord Derby as Under Secretary.
7   King George sends a message of congratulations to the troops in France.

9   E.S. Montagu appointed as Minister of Munitions.
Two German aeroplane raids on southeast coast (Dover and North Foreland) with no damage.

7   German submarine shells Seaham Harbour – 1 woman killed. Three armed trawlers sunk off Scottish coasts in action with German submarine.

12   8th Battalion involved in Somme battle.

13   Bank Holiday suspended. Allied conference on Munitions output held in London.
Bank rate 6%. German submarine sinks two trawlers and two fishing boats off Whitby.

17   Trade Unions recommend postponement of all holidays in connection with munitions production.
Daily cost of war now £6 million a day.

19   5th Battalion fighting in Delville Wood.

22   Silver badge granted for those disabled while serving in the armed forces.

23   1st /4th battalion attack near Pozieres on the Somme.

24   First Battalion Royal Berks fighting on the Somme.

27   Captain Charles Fryatt of the Great Eastern Liner *Brussels* is court-martialled and shot by German authorities in Belgium, for attempting to ram a German submarine.

28   Zeppelin raid on Lincolnshire and Norfolk – no casualties.

28   Prime Minister in House of Commons denounces murder of Captain Fryatt. Government contemplates immediate action.
H.E. Drake becomes Chief Secretary for Ireland.
Zeppelin raid on Norfolk, Suffolk, Cambridgeshire, Lincolnshire, Nottinghamshire and Kent – no casualties.

August

3   Prime Minister receives deputation from miners, railway men and transport workers for discussions about demobilisation problems after the war. Zeppelin raid on Norfolk, East Suffolk and Kent – no damage.
Sir Roger Casement hanged.

7   Admiralty deny allegation in German press that British hospital ships are being used as transport ships.

9   Zeppelin raid on Northern Counties and Norfolk – 10 killed and 16 injured.
10   Mr McKenna submitted a balance sheet to the Commons, based on the war continuing until 31 March 1917 – the country would be indebted by £3,440,000,000 with a national income of up to £2, 640,000,000.
     Premiere of the film *Battle of the Somme* at the Scala Theatre, London.
8   Seaplane raid on Dover – 7 injured.
21   The film *The Battle of the Somme* goes on general release.
22   Lloyd George gives survey of military situation and announces 35 Zeppelins destroyed by the Allies.
23   Zeppelin raid on East Suffolk – no casualties.
24   Zeppelin raid on East Suffolk, Essex, Kent and London – 9 killed and 40 injured.
25   Zeppelin raid on East and Southeast coast and London.

September
3   Thirteen airships raided the Midland and North Home Counties, Kent and London – 4 killed and 13 injured. Lt. William Leefe-Robinson was awarded the VC for shooting down one of the intruders over Cuffley, near Enfield.
5   At Birmingham the TUC insists on the restoration of trade union customs and practices after the war.
9   In Cardiff, South Wales railwaymen resolve to strike, demanding an increase of 10/- weekly on wages.
22   Aeroplane raid on Kent and Dover – no damage.
23   Big raid by German airships (probably 12) on London, Lincolnshire, Nottinghamshire, Norfolk and Kent. Two airships were brought down, one in flames. The second Zeppelin was set on fire by the crew before they surrendered; casualties due to the raid were 40 killed and 130 injured.
25   Seven airships raid Lancashire, Yorkshire and Lincolnshire – 43 killed and 31 injured.

October
1   L31 brought down at Potter's Bar after raid on the Midland and North Home Counties, Hertfordshire and London – 1 killed and 1 injured.

11   Mr Asquith delivers speech on 'No patched-up peace'.
16   Board of Trade issues average increase in retail prices of
     principal food articles between July 1914 and September 1916;
     overall increase 65 per cent.
22   Aeroplane raid on Sheerness – 2 injured.
23   Aeroplane raid on Margate – no injuries.
31   Increased wages demanded by Cardiff miners.

November
14   Pensions Bill introduced.
15   Appointment of Food Controller and control of bread
     foreshadowed. 8th Battalion fighting at Passchendaele.
17   Food regulations issued; Board of Trade invested with wide
     powers to prevent waste, regulate manufacture and production,
     direct sale and distribution, control markets, regulate price and
     commandeer any article.
20   Milk and flour regulations issued by Board of Trade.
23   German destroyers raid in the Channel at the north end of the
     Downs – little damage.
26   German naval raid near Lowestoft – armed trawler *Narval* sunk.
27   Zeppelin raid on Durham, Yorkshire, Staffordshire and Cheshire
–   two raiders brought down. Four people killed and 37 injured.
28   One aeroplane raids London at mid-day injuring 10 people. The
     aeroplane was subsequently shot down in France.
     Brixham fishing fleet attacked by German submarine.
29   The Board of Trade takes over the South Wales coalfield from 1
     December.
30   Lord Derby speaks on conditions for the New Volunteer Army –
     no man to lose civil employment and no compulsion to sign
     agreement, not to leave home save for defence of country.

December
1   Lloyd George states he is unable to remain in government because
     of his dissatisfaction with the leisurely conduct of the war.
3   Mr Asquith decides on reconstruction of government.
     Wage dispute in South Wales settled in favour of miners.
5   Lloyd George and Mr Asquith resign.

6   Cabinet crisis – Lloyd George asked to form administration.
      The Board of Agriculture is given powers to acquire land.
7   Lloyd George becomes Prime Minister.
9   New War Cabinet formed.
      Ministries of Food, Labour and Shipping formed.
11   Ministry of Labour comes into being.
14   Total cost of war so far: £1,950,000,000.
16   Government decides to take over Irish railways, to satisfaction of
      Irish people.
17   German Peace note received by the Foreign Office which lays the
      blame for the continuation of the war upon the Allied governments.
19   Lloyd George's first speech as Premier calls for the control of
      shipping, mining and food.
22   Ministries of Food, Pensions and shipping set up.
      King George's speech to Parliament urges the vigorous prosecution
      of the war until the security of Europe is firmly established.
31   Total air raid casualties for the year 311 killed and 752 injured.

Casualty List

Local area soldier casualties

It is not possible to give completely accurate figures for the number of men killed in any given locality. This is because records were not kept as accurately as they are today: some soldiers enlisted under false names and addresses, some made simple spelling mistakes – for example Charville not Charvil – while others provided few details, so no place of residence is recorded. In some cases this is rather strange. Take for example Three Mile Cross, a village that records no deaths in *Soldiers Died,* but there are two residents of the village listed on the Grazeley Trinity Church Memorial. This lists eighteen names while *Soldiers Died* only lists seven for Grazeley, with two from Three Mile Cross. Where do the remainder come from? For these reasons the CWGC records are incomplete, parish memorials often miss names off, simply because no one was aware of the death, while county boundary changes misplace many men. Complicating matters, many men are commemorated on more than one memorial, for example a school memorial, their regimental memorial as well as their town memorial.

In 1921, eighty-one volumes of *Soldiers Died in the Great War*, by regiment and corps, were published giving soldiers' names, rank, battalion or unit, place of birth, residence, place of enlistment, date of death and region in which they died, plus any military decorations awarded. An officers' volume was also produced. These have been supplemented in recent years by further local research, but the list is still incomplete.

Below, in tabular form, are details of soldier deaths. No officers are included as their official listings give no place of birth, for Reading and villages within a few miles radius – it is not an exhaustive list – merely a snapshot of losses. They are published with 'work in progress' status, being based on *Soldiers Died* and are necessarily incomplete.

These totals may disagree with the numbers on war memorials. However, these are often inaccurate as is clearly shown by the tables when the reader compares the three columns. This complexity is shown by the entries for Earley, which total forty-seven in *Soldiers Died* but St Peter's Church records the names of 112 local men who died. Is it possible that the difference is accounted for officers in all three arms plus naval and airmen? Unlikely, but possibly in apart, as there are no lists for the Royal Navy and Royal Air Force. One man listed on the Earley memorial was a sailor and lived in Australia so would be included on their official list of losses but is recorded in Earley where he was born.

The numbers make interesting reading when compared to the total deaths for Great Britain, and also when resident deaths are compared against the deaths of those born in the town or village. In October 2013, fifty-three villages were identified as 'Thankful' or 'Blessed Villages'; settlements in England and Wales from which all their then members of the armed forces survived the war. No village in Scotland or Ireland is classed as a 'Thankful Village'. Similarly, no village in Berkshire is classed as 'Blessed' but some, like Riseley, Sonning Eye and Winnersh register no deaths on *Soldiers Died.* Without easy access to naval and air force deaths it is difficult to know whether these villages should be included as 'Blessed Villages'. Recent research has added and taken villages off the list.

Recording deaths on memorials was not an easy matter. Should it be residents, who may have only been there a short time, or those born in the town or village? Some may have family still living there but they had moved on, or even left the country, while some families simply wanted to forget and did not get involved. Then of course there were those who died after the memorial had been consecrated and may not be recorded and those who their loved ones still believed might be missing as the requests for information showed. 'Can any returned prisoner from Germany give information regarding Sapper A. Cook, No. 137828 8th Division 15th Field Co. R.E.'s, missing since 27 May 1918? Any news concerning him would be gratefully received by his wife at 68, Watlington Street, Reading.'

It is also interesting to compare official statistics against the deaths reported in the papers, through official casualty lists. Perhaps one day there will be an accurate record for Reading.

Soldiers died in Reading			
Year of death	Resident	Born in Reading	Born & resident
1914	32	65	2
1915	95	196	14
1916	93	273	5
Total	220	534	21

The first resident to die was Reginald Haines who died of wounds on 14 September 1914 serving with 1 Dorsets. William Willoughby was the first soldier to die who had been born in Reading. He died on 23 August 1914 serving with 1 Royal Scots Fusiliers.

Soldiers died in Arborfield			
Year of death	Resident	Born in Arborfield	Born & resident
1914	0	1	0
1915	1	3	0
1916	0	0	0
Total	1	4	0

Soldiers died in Barkham			
Year of death	Resident	Born in Barkham	Born & resident
1914	0	1	0
1915	0	1	0
1916	1	1	0
Total	1	3	0

Soldiers died in Bearwood			
Year of death	Resident	Born in Bearwood	Born & resident
1914	0	0	0
1915	0	0	0
1916	0	2	0
Total	0	2	0

Soldiers died in Burghfield			
Year of death	Resident	Born in Burghfield	Born & resident
1914	2	0	0
1915	0	8	0
1916	2	3	1
Total	4	11	1

Soldiers died in Burghfield Common			
Year of death	Resident	Born in Burghfield Common	Born & resident
1914	0	0	0
1915	0	0	0
1916	0	0	0
Total	0	0	0

Soldiers died in Calcot			
Year of death	Resident	Born in Calcot	Born & resident
1914	0	0	0
1915	0	0	0
1916	0	2	0
Total	0	2	0

Soldiers died in Caversham			
Year of death	Resident	Born in Caversham	Born & resident
1914	2	1	0
1915	14	16	3
1916	18	22	5
Total	65	39	8

Soldiers died in Charvil			
Year of death	Resident	Born in Charvil	Born & resident
1914	0	0	0
1915	0	0	0
1916	0	1	0
Total	0	1	0

Soldiers died in Coley			
Year of death	Resident	Born in Coley	Born & resident
1914	1	0	0
1915	2	2	1
1916	0	0	0
Total	3	2	1

Soldiers died in Dunsden

Year of death	Resident	Born in Dunsden	Born & resident
1914	1	1	0
1915	1	0	0
1916	1	2	0
Total	3	3	0

Soldiers died in Dunsden Green

Year of death	Resident	Born in Dunsden Green	Born & resident
1914	1	0	0
1915	0	0	0
1916	0	0	0
Total	1	0	0

Soldiers died in Earley

Year of death	Resident	Born in Earley	Born & resident
1914	0	0	0
1915	0	3	0
1916	0	3	0
Total	3	23	1

Soldiers died in Grazeley

Year of death	Resident	Born in Grazeley	Born & resident
1914	0	0	0
1915	0	0	0
1916	3	2	0
Total	3	2	0

Soldiers died in Grazeley Green

Year of death	Resident	Born in Grazeley Green	Born & resident
1914	0	0	0
1915	0	0	0
1916	0	0	0
Total	0	0	0

Soldiers died in Hurst			
Year of death	Resident	Born in Hurst	Born & resident
1914	1	2	1
1915	3	1	1
1916	1	10	0
Total	5	13	2

Soldiers died in Kidmore End			
Year of death	Resident	Born in Kidmore End	Born & resident
1914	1	0	0
1915	2	0	0
1916	1	0	0
Total	4	0	0

Soldiers died in Maple Durham			
Year of death	Resident	Born in Maple Durham	Born & resident
1914	0	0	0
1915	0	0	0
1916	2	3	0
Total	2	3	0

Soldiers died in Mortimer			
Year of death	Resident	Born in Mortimer	Born & resident
1914	3	1	1
1915	10	9	5
1916	9	9	4
Total	22	19	10

Soldiers died in Shinfield			
Year of death	Resident	Born in Shinfield	Born & resident
1914	2	3	1
1915	1	1	0
1916	0	3	0
Total	3	7	1

Soldiers died in Shiplake			
Year of death	Resident	Born in Shiplake	Born & resident
1914	0	0	0
1915	1	0	0
1916	0	3	0
Total	1	3	0

Soldiers died in Sindlesham			
Year of death	Resident	Born in Sindlesham	Born & resident
1914	0	0	0
1915	0	0	0
1916	0	0	0
Total	0	0	0

Soldiers died in Sonning			
Year of death	Resident	Born in Sonning	Born & resident
1914	0	1	0
1915	0	0	0
1916	4	3	0
Total	4	4	0

Soldiers died in Sonning Common			
Year of death	Resident	Born in Sonning Common	Born & resident
1914	0	0	0
1915	0	0	0
1916	0	0	0
Total	0	0	0

Soldiers died in Swallowfield			
Year of death	Resident	Born in Swallowfield	Born & resident
1914	1	0	0
1915	2	3	0
1916	1	5	0
Total	4	8	0

Soldiers died in Theale			
Year of death	Resident	Born in Theale	Born & resident
1914	2	0	0
1915	1	1	0
1916	8	5	4
Total	11	6	4

Soldiers died in Tilehurst			
Year of death	Resident	Born in Tilehurst	Born & resident
1914	2	3	0
1915	11	7	2
1916	7	12	5
Total	20	22	7

Soldiers died in Twyford			
Year of death	Resident	Born in Twyford	Born & resident
1914	4	0	0
1915	7	6	1
1916	10	3	1
Total	21	9	2

Soldiers died in Wargrave			
Year of death	Resident	Born in Wargrave	Born & resident
1914	1	0	0
1915	1	6	1
1916	3	4	0
Total	5	10	1

Soldiers died in Whitley			
Year of death	Resident	Born in Whitley	Born & resident
1914	0	0	0
1915	1	0	0
1916	3	0	0
Total	4	0	0

Soldiers died in Woodley			
Year of death	Resident in Woodley	Born in Woodley	Born & resident
1914	1	1	0
1915	0	0	0
1916	2	3	2
Total	3	4	2

Bibliography

Adkin, F.J. *From the ground up*. Airlife. 1983

Ashworth, C. *Action Stations 9 Military airfields of the Central South and South-East*. Patrick Stevens. 1985.

Barnes-Phillips, D. *So many hearts make a school: The centenary of the George Palmer Schools, Reading*. Corridor Press. 2007.

Barnes-Phillips, D. *This is our school. Reading British School 1811-2011*. Corridor Press. 2011.

BFWI. *Berkshire within living memory*. Countryside Books & BFWI. 1996.

Bishop, M. 'Bats, Balls and Biscuits'. Cricket Heritage Project, University of Huddersfield. 2008.

Booker, F. *The Great Western Railway*. David and Charles. 1977.

Charles, B. 'Crime and Calamity in Cholsey'. www.lulu.com. 2013.

Corley, T. *Quaker Enterprise in Biscuits*. Hutchinson & Co. 1972.

Cruttwell, C.R.M.F. *The war service of the 1/4th Royal Berkshire Regiment (T.F.)*. Basil Blackwell. 1922.

Cull, I. *The 2nd Battalion Royal Berkshire Regiment in WW1*. Tempus. 2005.

Dearing, J. *The church that would not die*. Baron Birch. 1993.

Dormer, E.W. *The Story of the Royal Berkshire Hospital*. Poynder Press. 1937.

Downs, D. *Biscuits and Royals*. Fericon Press Ltd. 1984.

Earley Local History Group. *Suttons Seeds A History 1806-2006*. Earley Local History Group. 2006.

Eddlestone, J. J. *Foul deeds and suspicious deaths in Reading*. Wharncliffe. 2009.

Farrar, H. *The Book of Hurst*. Barracuda Books. 1984.

Fowler, Rev. Canon. W. 'St Peter's Magazine 1917-18'. No publisher. 1919.

Gray, R and Argyle, C. Chronicle of the First World War Volume 1, 1914 – 1916. Facts on File, 1991.

Gray, R and Argyle, C. *Chronicle of the First World War* Volume 2, 1917 – 1921. Facts on File, 1991.

Handscomb, S. *Tilehurst*. Berkshire Books. 1996.

Hylton, S. *A Reading Century*. Sutton Publishing. 1999.

Jeator, A. *The British Red Cross in Berkshire 1907 to 2007*. The British Red Cross. 2007

Ministry of Information. *Chronology of the war*. Constable & Co. Ltd. 1919.

Oakes, J and Parsons. *Old School Ties*. DSM. 2001.

Oakes, J. *Kitchener's Lost Boys*. The History Press. 2009.

Perkins, A. *The book of Sonning*. Baron. 1999.

Petre, F.L. 'The Royal Berkshire Regiment Volume 2 1914 – 1918'. Royal Gloucestershire, Berkshire and Wiltshire Regiment Wardrobe and Museum Trust. 2004.

Phillips, D. Berkshire, *A County History*. Countryside Books. 1993.

Railton, M. and Barr, M. 'Battle Workhouse and Hospital 1867-2005'. Berkshire Medical Heritage Centre. 2005.

Railton, M. and Barr, M. 'The Royal Berkshire Hospital 1939-1989'. The Royal Berkshire Hospital. 1989.

Rooke, P. Redlands *A hundred years at school*. Reading Schools PTA. 1991.

Southern, P. *The story of a prison*. Osprey. 1975.

The *Berkshire Chronicle*

The *Reading Mercury*

The *Reading Observer*

The *Reading Standard*

Trigg, J. 'A County at War Berkshire 1914-1918'. www.johntrigg.org.uk 2007.

Vaughan, A. *Grime and Glory*. John Murray. 1985.

Woodhouse, L. Downs, D. Witts, I. Brown, G. *Wilson School 100 years of memories*. Corridor Press. 2006.

Websites

http://www.spartacus.schoolnet.co.uk/FWWantigerman.htm

http://www.thedorsetpage.com/history/vc/james_welch.htm

Index